𝔇𝔞𝔦𝔩𝔶 𝔗𝔢𝔩𝔢𝔤𝔯𝔞𝔭𝔥

POCKET SPORTS FACTS

FLAT RACING

TONY STAFFORD

𝕿

Consultant Editor: Norman Barrett

Editor: Gill Freeman

Design: Nigel Standerline

Designed and produced by
Autumn Publishing Ltd.,
10 Eastgate Square, Chichester,
West Sussex.

Published by Telegraph Publications,
135, Fleet Street,
London EC4P 4BL

Acknowledgements
Race form Up-to-Date
Sporting Life
Timeform
Queen Anne Press

© 1984 Daily Telegraph
   and Autumn Publishing Ltd.

Typesetting by Project Reprographics, Chichester.
Printed by CGP Delo, Yugoslavia.

ISBN 0 86367 018 0

Cover picture: Steve Cauthen
*Picture credits: Colorsport; All-Sport;
Syndication International; A.M.P.S.;
Selwyn Photos; David Hastings; Sport and
General.*

CONTENTS

INTRODUCTION

Tony Stafford

Great Britain may no longer be a first rate world power
politically, but in the international arena, British horse racing
is very much in the forefront.

In recent years investment from abroad in the British racing
scene has grown rapidly. Thus while many other industries are
in decline, horse racing, breeding and their many allied
activities are relatively strong.

The life blood of racing has always been betting, and the
revenue from both the betting and the breeding industries has
become a major contributor to the nation's coffers.

Yet for all its omni-presence and its familiarity as an activity
with the public, much of what happens behind the scenes in
racing is not well known or understood.

The Daily Telegraph Pocket Sports Facts on Racing is aimed
at providing the reader with a better insight into racing at all
levels, dealing with the development of the sport into an
industry and concentrating on such vital areas as the Classics,
around which the whole pattern of racing revolves.

Britain and Ireland, like the Blue Grasslands of Kentucky
which have enjoyed parallel development, have ideal land
for the breeding and rearing of the thoroughbred. The major
rearing and training centres, usually limestone based, are
conducive to the provision of strong bone, a vital factor if a
horse is going to be strong enough to cope with the stresses
involved in galloping at around 40 miles per hour.

Racing developed most readily around the Newmarket area
on the famous Heath which today still houses a large number
of training stables and stud farms as well as the most extensive
and varied galloping grounds.

The influx of very wealthy owners, notably from the Middle
East, has indeed strengthened the development of
Newmarket, which also houses the most important sales in
Britain. Here the yearlings and foals which will become the
two-year-olds of the following years are paraded and sold in a
critical arena in which good pedigree and sound conformation
are the vital factors.

During the last decade, the market for bloodstock has been
characterised by a steady—sometimes violent—upsurge. The
arrival on the scene of the free-spending Arab owners, who
can compete with the existing traditional big buyers has
heightened competition.

World stallion values have also soared, so much so that by
1983, Shareef Dancer, despite a far from flawless racing
record, but with a Classic win in Ireland and a highly
fashionable pedigree, was syndicated for 40 million dollars
(£26 million).

The presence of such wealthy owners in Britain has reversed
the long-standing trend by which the most valuable stallions
were almost guaranteed to be exported to the United States.
Now Europeans and others with businesses based here, can
outbid the Americans, so many top stallions remain at stud in

Ireland or England.

When immediately before and after the last world war many top European horses were exported to the United States, there was an outcry. Time has shown that the pessimists were right, for without such exportations, the mighty Northern Dancer line—the most influential in the world today—would not have been founded. Now the might is on this side of the Atlantic.

The first thing you notice when undertaking a book of this type is the immense scope of the subject. Athletics, on the world stage, peaks on such major events as the Olympic Games every four years. Golf has its major championships, cricket its test matches.

For the most part the competitors in these major sports are around for a long time.

But in racing, the jockeys and trainers stay in evidence for many years. Most top riding careers, for example, extend for 30 years or more, while a trainer can hold a licence even longer. Horses though are much more ephemeral, and a flat-racer that enjoys three full seasons of success is a rarity.

There are so many races, too. The top horses have the Classics, five races each year, two restricted to fillies, but there are many other major events in which a horse can gain an international reputation and thus acquire great value.

The true champion, like Nijinsky, who won the Triple Crown—only the second horse since the end of World War One—of 2,000 Guineas, Derby and St Leger before going on to a stallion career equally glittering, really earns the accolade.

The business of the racing and breeding industry—the improvement of the breed—is the underlying essence of a sport which means many different things to the many who work in or are entertained by it. We hope this book helps your understanding and enjoyment of a great sport.

Nijinsky, winner of the Triple Crown in 1970

THE CLASSICS

John Randall

The five Classic races might have been deliberately designed
as a coherent programme to test both the speed and stamina
of the three-year-old equine élite at the appropriate stae of
their physical development; over a mile in the spring, a mile
and a half in the summer and an extended mile and threequarters in the autumn.

The Classics might have been so designed, but they weren't.
At the time of the founding of the St Leger (1776), Oaks (1779),
Derby (1780), 2000 Guineas (1809) and 1000 Guineas (1814)—
and for many years after—there was no organised pattern to
the sport in England. Racing at Doncaster, Epsom and
Newmarket developed independently, and it was not until the
latter half of the 19th century that the five races, which had
originally been of humble status, were connected and had the
word 'Classic' applied to them.

Two centuries ago horse racing was still at an early stage of
its development. The most common type of contest was the
match race run in heats of up to four miles, and it was quite
usual for there to be only one or two such events per afternoon
since the day's sporting programme might also include
hunting, cock-fighting, card-playing, prize-fights and other
inducements to gamble. Trainers and jockeys were lowly
grooms employed by the owners and their names would not
have been regarded as worth recording by the sporting
newspapers—had there been any.

Horses were not retired until their merit had been rigorously
tested but demands were not made on them until they were
fully mature. Eclipse, who had been at stud for six seasons
when the St Leger was first run, retired undefeated after a
career of 18 races yet was not seen in public until he was five.

THE ST LEGER

When Colonel St Leger, one of the stewards at Doncaster
races, suggested that the course follow a recent trend by
staging a contest confined to three-year-olds in 1776, no-one
could have predicted that it would be seen in retrospect as the
oldest Classic in the world. A prize for such immature animals
could not hope to attract a field of distinction, and even
among the few races for three-year-olds run in England that
season Doncaster's was among the least valuable.

For the first two years the new race did not even have a title,
being known simply as the £25 sweepstakes, and it was run
over two miles on Cantley Common. The inaugural edition
was won by an unnamed filly owned by the Marquess of
Rockingham, a great supporter of racing in Yorkshire.

After the 1777 meeting the local stewards, town councillors
and other worthies held a dinner at the Red Lion, the foremost
inn in Doncaster, to discuss the following year's programme. It
was suggested that the sweepstakes be named the
Rockingham Stakes but the Marquess declined, saying that it

had been Colonel St Leger's brainchild and that it should bear his name. The first race under the title of the St Leger was therefore run in 1778 over the new course on Town Moor; it was won by a grey filly, Hollandaise.

Anthony St Leger, who lived nearby at Park Hill, later became a lieutenant-general, but neither he nor any member of his family looms large in the history of the Turf. He would be totally forgotten today had the race, which was so casually named after him, not attained such prominence in later years.

By 1800 the Doncaster meeting was the premier social event of the year in the north. The aristocracy and gentry from far around rented houses in the town and racing was only one of the week's entertainments, the others including plays, concerts, dinners, balls and many sporting diversions.

However, during the first two or three decades of the 19th century racing became the focus of Doncaster week and the St Leger caught the imgination of the public, being matched by the Derby alone in its esteem. The distance was reduced from two miles to 1m 6f 193yds in 1813 and to 1m 6f 132yds in 1826, by which time it was commonly referred to, even in the Racing Calendar, as the Great St Leger.

THE DERBY AND THE OAKS

Although Epsom was the scene of Eclipse's first public appearance, the Surrey course was of minor importance in the 18th century and there were certainly no fanfares of trumpets when the Oaks and the Derby were inaugurated. They were not even the first sweepstakes for three-year-olds run at Epsom, such races having been held there twice in the mid-1770s.

Both Epsom Classics owe their existence to Edward Stanley, 12th Earl of Derby, who was one of the chief supporters of racing there and had a country house a few miles away called The Oaks. After the 1778 meeting Lord Derby and the members of his house-party decided on a new race for three-year-old fillies over 1½ miles, to be held the following year. Bridget, the first winner of the Oaks Stakes, was owned by Lord Derby himself.

The success of the race encouraged Lord Derby and his guests, among whom was Sir Charles Bunbury the leading light of the Jockey Club, to arrange a similar event for colts the next year. There is no evidence to support the story of the two men tossing a coin to decide whether the race should be called the Derby or the Bunbury but, whatever the truth about its origins, the first Derby Stakes was run over a mile on 4 May 1780; the victor, Diomed, earned 1,075 guineas for his owner, who happened to be Sir Charles Bunbury. The distance was increased to 1½ miles in 1784.

Diomed was an outstanding horse but the same cannot be said of most of the early Derby winners. Nevertheless the importance of the race grew until, by its 50th anniversary, it was widely regarded as the sport's premier prize—though northerners would have accorded first place to the St Leger. The Oaks kept pace with its younger companion-race and became easily the most important event in the Calendar confined to fillies.

Betting on the Derby started almost a year in advance and on the big day itself Parliament would adjourn so that its members could join the many thousands thronging to the course in a carnival atmosphere. The Derby's prestige was such that in 1848 Benjamin Disraeli, not himself a racing man, spoke of it as the 'Blue Riband of the Turf'.

Unfortunately this status attracted bribery, nobbling and other acts of villainy which reached their peak in the 1844 Derby. Running Rein was first past the post but was exposed as a four-year-old by Lord George Bentinck, then the most influential man in racing, though it is likely that this 'ringer' was by no means the first horse older than three to win the Derby.

Until the revolution in transport brought about by the railways in the early Victorian era, few horses contested both the Derby and the St Leger. Horses had to travel to every meeting on foot—a trailer was first used in 1816 but the idea did not catch on—so to a large extent the southern and northern circuits were separate and Epsom heroes seldom ventured as far as Doncaster. Of the first 68 winners of the Derby only one, Champion in 1800, went on to success in the St Leger.

THE TWO THOUSAND AND ONE THOUSAND GUINEAS

Newmarket, the main centre of racing in England since the days of Charles II, has been the home of the Jockey Club since 1752 but its two Classics are of comparatively recent origin. The 2000 Guineas over the Rowley Mile was inaugurated in 1809 and the fillies' equivalent, the 1000 Guineas, followed five years later.

Initially of no more than average importance among the prizes at the Headquarters of racing, they were soon recognised as significant trials for the Derby and Oaks respectively, and ultimately became Classics in their own right.

THE TRIPLE CROWN

A hundred years ago the five Classics had assumed approximately their present status and were beginning to be regarded as a series of races. The phrase 'Triple Crown' to denote the three colts' Classics—the 2000 Guineas, Derby and St Leger—was coined around 1870 so that West Australian (1853), Gladiateur (1865) and Lord Lyon (1866) became the first three Triple Crown winners only in retrospect.

FACTS AND FEATS

Finally, a few Classic facts and feats. The largest margin of victory was achieved by Mayonaise when winning the 1000 Guineas by 20 lengths in 1859 while Pretty Polly's SP for the Oaks in 1904 was 8/100. The biggest field was 34 for the 1862 Derby whereas Tontine was able to walk over for the 1000 Guineas in 1825.

The unluckiest loser was undoubtedly Craganour, first past the post in both the 2000 Guineas and Derby in 1913 but robbed by a judge's mistake in the first instance (by no means the only such blunder before the introduction of the photo-finish camera) and by the stewards in the second. He thus followed Running Rein as the second Derby winner to be disqualified.

James Croft of Middleham saddled four horses for the St Leger in 1822 and they filled the first four places—an achievement unmatched till Michael Dickinson's five in last year's Cheltenham Gold Cup. Another Yorkshire trainer, John Scott of Malton, sent out the winners of 41 Classics between 1827 and 1863 and Frank Buckle holds the jockeys' record with 27 wins between 1792 and 1827 that we can be certain about, though contemporary accounts are incomplete and he probably rode a total of 29.

As for the identity of the best-ever winner, there is no answer that would not be contentious since nearly every great racehorse trained in England appears on the Classic roll of honour. Fashion dictates that modern champions need prove themselves only at middle distances, but the five Classics have stood the test of time and remain the definitive measure of excellence in the thoroughbred.

Frank Buckle rode at least 27 classic winners between 1792 and 1827

WINNERS OF THE GREAT RACES

THE CLASSICS

THE DERBY

Epsom 1½m 3-y-o

* Run at Newmarket

1780	Diomed	1820	Sailor
1781	Young Eclipse	1821	Gustavus
1782	Assassin	1822	Moses
1783	Saltram	1823	Emilius
1784	Serjeant	1824	Cedric
1785	Aimwell	1825	Middleton
1786	Noble	1826	Lap-dog
1787	Sir Peter Teazle	1827	Mameluke
1788	Sir Thomas	1828	Cadland
1789	Skyscraper	1829	Frederick
1790	Rhadamanthus	1830	Priam
1791	Eager	1831	Spaniel
1792	John Bull	1832	St Giles
1793	Waxy	1833	Dangerous
1794	Daedalus	1834	Plenipotentiary
1795	Spread Eagle	1835	Mundig
1796	Didelot	1836	Middleton
1797	br c by Fidget	1837	Phosphorus
1798	Sir Harry	1838	Amato
1799	Archduke	1839	Bloomsbury
1800	Champion	1840	Little Wonder
1801	Eleanor	1841	Coronation
1802	Tyrant	1842	Attila
1803	Ditto	1843	Cotherstone
1804	Hannibal	1844	Orlando
1805	Cardinal Beaufort	1845	The Merry Monarch
1806	Paris	1846	Pyrrhus the First
1807	Election	1847	The Cossack
1808	Pan	1848	Surplice
1809	Pope	1849	The Flying Dutchman
1810	Whalebon	1850	Voltigeur
1811	Phantom	1851	Teddington
1812	Octavius	1852	Daniel O'Rourke
1813	Smolensko	1853	West Australian
1814	Blucher	1854	Andover
1815	Whisker	1855	Wild Dayrell
1816	Prince Leopold	1856	Ellington
1817	Azor	1857	Blink Bonny
1818	Sam	1858	Beadsman
1819	Tiresias	1859	Musjid

Year	Winner		Year	Winner
1860	Thormanby		1902	Ard Patrick
1861	Kettledrum		1903	Rock Sand
1862	Caractacus		1904	St Amant
1863	Macaroni		1905	Cicero
1864	Blair Athol		1906	Spearmint
1865	Gladiateur		1907	Orby
1866	Lord Lyon		1908	Signorinetta
1867	Hermit		1909	Minoru
1868	Blue Gown		1910	Lemberg
1868	Pretender		1911	Sunstar
1869	Pretender		1912	Tagalie
1870	Kingcraft		1913	Aboyeur
1871	Favonius		1914	Durbar Ii
1872	Cremorne		1915*	Pommern
1873	Doncaster		1916*	Fifinella
1874	George Frederick		1917*	Gay Crusader
1875	Galopin		1918*	Gainsborough
1876	Kisber		1919	Grand Parade
1877	Silvio		1920	Spion Kop
1878	Sefton		1921	Humorist
1879	Sir Bevy		1922	Capt Cuttle
1880	Bend Or		1923	Papyrus
1881	Iroquois		1924	Sansovino
1882	Shotover		1925	Manna
1883	St Blaise		1926	Coronach
1884	Gatien		1927	Call Boy
1884	Harvester		1928	Felstead
1885	Melton		1929	Trigo
1886	Ormonde		1930	Blenheim
1887	Merry Hampton		1931	Cameronian
1888	Ayrshire		1932	April the Fifth
1889	Donovan		1933	Hyperion
1890	Sainfoin		1934	Windsor Lad
1891	Common		1935	Bahram
1892	Sir Hugo		1936	Mahmoud
1893	Isinglass		1937	Mid-day Sun
1894	Ladas		1938	Bois Roussel
1895	Sir Visto		1939	Blue Peter
1896	Persimmon		1940*	Pont l'Eveque
1897	Galtee More		1941*	Owen Tudor
1898	Jeddah		1942*	Watling Street
1899	Flying Fox		1943*	Straight Deal
1900	Diamond Jubilee		1944*	Ocean Swell
1901	Volodvovski		1945*	Dante

Year	Winner	Trainer	Jockey	SP
1946	Airborne	R Perryman	T Lowrey	50-1
1947	Pearl Diver	C Halsey	G Bridgland	40-1
1948	My Love	R Carver	W Johnstone	100-9

		Trainer	Jockey	SP
1949	**Nimbus**	G Colling	E C Elliott	7-1
1950	**Galcador**	C Semblat	W Johnstone	100-9
1951	**Arctic Prince**	W Stephenson	C Spares	28-1
1952	**Tulyar**	M Marsh	C Smirke	11-2
1953	**Pinza**	N Bertie	G Richards	5-1
1954	**Never Say Die**	J Lawson	L Piggott	33-1
1955	**Phil Drake**	F Mathet	F Palmer	100-8
1956	**Lavandin**	A Head	W Johnstone	7-1
1957	**Crepello**	N Murless	L Piggott	6-4
1958	**Hard Ridden**	J Rogers	C Smirke	18-1
1959	**Parthia**	C B-Rochfort	W Carr	10-1
1960	**St Paddy**	N Murless	L Piggott	7-1
1961	**Psidium**	H Wragg	R Poincelet	66-1
1962	**Larkspur**	M V O'Brien	N Sellwood	22-1
1963	**Relko**	F Mathet	Y Saint-Martin	5-1
1964	**Santa Claus**	J Rogers	A Breasley	15-8
1965	**Sea Bird II**	E Pollett	T P Glennon	7-4
1966	**Charlottown**	G Smyth	A Breasley	5-1
1967	**Royal Palace**	N Murless	G Moore	7-4
1968	**Sir Ivor**	M V O'Brien	L Piggott	4-5
1969	**Blakeney**	A Budgett	E Johnson	15-2
1970	**Nijinsky**	M V O'Brien	L Piggott	11-8
1971	**Mill Reef**	I Balding	G Lewis	100-30
1972	**Roberto**	M V O'Brien	L Piggott	3-1
1973	**Morston**	A Budgett	E Hide	25-1
1974	**Snow Knight**	P Nelson	B Taylor	50-1
1975	**Grundy**	P Walwyn	P Eddery	5-1
1976	**Empery**	M Zilber	L Piggott	10-1
1977	**The Minstrel**	M V O'Brien	L Piggott	5-1
1978	**Shirley Heights**	J Dunlop	G Starkey	8-1
1979	**Troy**	W Hern	W Carson	6-1
1980	**Henbit**	W Hern	W Carson	7-1
1981	**Shergar**	M Stoute	W R Swinburn	10-11
1982	**Golden Fleece**	M V O'Brien	P Eddery	3-1
1983	**Teenoso**	G Wragg	L Piggott	9-2

ONE THOUSAND GUINEAS

Newmarket 1m 3-y-o

* New One Thousand Guineas on July course.

1814	**Charlotte**	1821	**Zeal**
1815	**filly by Sclim**	1822	**Whizgig**
1816	**Rhoda**	1823	**Zinc**
1817	**Neva**	1824	**Cobweb**
1818	**Corinne**	1825	**Tontine**
1819	**Catgut**	1826	**Problem**
1820	**Rowena**	1827	**Arab**

1828	Zoe	1879	Wheel of Fortune
1829	Mouse	1880	Elizabeth
1830	Charlotte West	1881	Thebais
1831	Galantine	1882	St Marguerite
1832	Galata	1883	Hauteur
1833	Tarantella	1884	Busybody
1834	May Day	1885	Farewell
1835	Preserve	1886	Miss Jummy
1836	Destiny	1887	Reve d'Or
1837	Chapeau d'Espagne	1888	Briar-root
1838	Barcarolle	1889	Minthe
1839	Cara	1890	Semolina
1840	Crucifix	1891	Mimi
1841	Potentia	1892	La Fleche
1842	Firebrand	1893	Siffleuse
1843	Extempore	1894	Amiable
1844	Sorella	1895	Galeottia
1845	Pic-nic	1896	Thais
1846	Mendicant	1897	Chelandry
1847	Clementina	1898	Nun Nicer
1848	Canezou	1899	Sibola
1849	Flea	1900	Winifreda
1850	Filly by Slane	1901	Aida
1851	Aphrodite	1902	Sceptre
1852	Kate	1903	Quintessence
1853	Mentmore Lass	1904	Pretty Polly
1854	Virago	1905	Cherry Lass
1855	Habena	1906	Flair
1856	Manganese	1907	Witch Elm
1857	Imperieuse	1908	Rhodora
1858	Governess	1909	Electra
1859	Mayonaise	1910	Winkipop
1860	Sagitta	1911	Atmah
1861	Nemesis	1912	Tagalie
1862	Hurricane	1913	Jest
1863	Lady Augusta	1914	Princess Dorrie
1864	Tomato	1915	Vaucluse
1865	Siberia	1916	Canyon
1866	Repulse	1917	Diadem
1867	Achievement	1918	Ferry
1868	Formosa	1919	Roseway
1869	Scottish Queen	1920	Cinna
1870	Hester	1921	Bettina
1871	Hannah	1922	Silver Urn
1872	Reine	1923	Tranquil
1873	Cecilia	1924	Plack
1874	Apology	1925	Saucy Sue
1875	Spinaway	1926	Pillion
1876	Camelia	1927	Cresta Run
1877	Belphoebe	1928	Scuttle
1878	Pilgrimage	1929	Taj Mah

1930	Fair Isle	1938		Rockfel
1931	Four Course	1939		Galatea II
1932	Kandy	1940	*	Godiva
1933	Brown Betty	1941	*	Dancing Time
1934	Campanula	1942	*	Sun Chariot
1935	Mesa	1943	*	Herringbone
1936	Tide-way	1944	*	Picture Play
1937	Exhibitionnist	1945	*	Sun Stream

		Trainer	Jockey	SP
1946	Hypericum	C B-Rochfort	D Smith	100-6
1947	Imprudence	J Lieux	W Johnstone	4-1
1948	Queenpot	N Murless	G Richards	6-1
1949	Musidora	C Elsey	E Britt	100-8
1950	Camaree	A Lieux	W Johnstone	10-1
1951	Belle Of All	N Bertie	G Richards	4-1
1952	Zabara	V Smyth	K Gethin	7-1
1953	Happy Laughter	J Jarvis	E Mercer	10-1
1954	Festoon	N Cannon	A Breasley	9-2
1955	Meld	C B-Rochfort	W Carr	11-4
1956	Honeylight	C Elsey	E Britt	100-6
1957	Rose Royale	A Head	C Smirke	6-1
1958	Bella Paola	F Mathet	S Boullenger	8-11
1959	Petite Etoile	N Murless	D Smith	8-1
1960	Never Too Late	E Pollet	R Poincelet	8-11
1961	Sweet Solera	R Day	W Rickaby	4-1
1962	Abermaid	H Wragg	W Williamson	100-6
1963	Hula Dancer	E Pollet	R Poincelet	1-2
1964	Pourparler	PJ Prendergast	G Bourgoure	11-2
1965	Night Off	W Wharton	W Williamson	9-2
1966	Glad Rags	MV O'Brien	P Cook	100-6
1967	Fleet	N Murless	G Moore	11-2
1968	Caergwrie	N Murless	A Barclay	4-1
1969	Full Dress II	H Wragg	R Hutchinson	7-1
1970	Humble Duty	P Walwyn	L Piggott	3-1
1971	Altesse Royale	N Murless	Y Saint-Martin	25-1
1972	Waterloo	JW Watts	E Hide	8-1
1973	Mysterious	N Murless	G Lewis	11-1
1974	Highclere	W Hern	J Mercer	12-1
1975	Nocturnal Spree	HVS Murless	J Roe	14-1
1976	Flying Water	A Penna	Y Saint-Martin	2-1
1977	Mrs McArdy	MW Easterby	E Hide	16-1
1978	Enstone Spark	B Hills	E Johnson	35-1
1979	One In A Million	H Cecil	J Mercer	Evens
1980	Quick As Lightning	J Dunlop	B Rouse	12-1
1981	Fairy Footsteps	H Cecil	L Piggott	6-4
1982	On The House	H Wragg	J Reid	33-1
1983	Ma Biche	Mme C Head	F Head	5-2

TWO THOUSAND GUINEAS

Newmarket 1m 3-y-o

* New Two Thousand Guineas on July Course.

1809	Wizard	1855	Lord of the Isles
1810	Hephestion	1856	Fazzoletto
1811	Trophonius	1857	Vedette
1812	Cwrw	1858	Fitz-Roland
1813	Smolensko	1859	The Promised Land
1814	Olive	1860	The Wizard
1815	Tigris	1861	Diophantus
1816	Nectar	1862	The Marquis
1817	Manfred	1863	Macaroni
1818	Interpreter	1864	General Peel
1819	Antar	1865	Gladiateur
1820	Pindarrie	1866	Lord Lyon
1821	Reginald	1867	Vauban
1822	Pastille	1868	Moslem
1823	Nicolo		Formosa
1824	Schahriar	1869	Pretender
1825	Enamel	1870	Macgregor
1826	Dervise	1871	Bothwell
1827	Turcoman	1872	Prince Charlie
1828	Cadland	1873	Gang Forward
1829	Patron	1874	Atlantic
1830	Augustus	1875	Camballo
1831	Riddlesworth	1876	Petrarch
1832	Archibald	1877	Chamant
1833	Clearwell	1878	Pilgrimage
1834	Glencoe	1879	Charibert
1835	Ibrahim	1880	Petronel
1836	Bay Middleton	1881	Peregrine
1837	Achmet	1882	Shotover
1838	Grey Momus	1883	Galliard
1839	The Corsair	1884	Scot Free
1840	Crucifix	1885	Paradox
1841	Ralph	1886	Ormonde
1842	Meteor	1887	Enterprise
1843	Cotherstone	1888	Ayrshire
1844	The Ugly Buck	1889	Enthusiast
1845	Idas	1890	Surefoot
1846	Sir Tatton Sykes	1891	Common
1847	Conyngham	1892	Bonavista
1848	Flatcatcher	1893	Isinglass
1849	Nunnykirk	1894	Ladas
1850	Pitsford	1895	Kirkconnel
1851	Hernandez	1896	St Frusquin
1852	Stockwell	1897	Galtee More
1853	West Australian	1898	Disraeli
1854	The Hermit	1899	Flying Fox

1900	**Diamond Jubilee**	1923	**Ellangowan**
1901	**Handicapper**	1924	**Diophon**
1902	**Sceptre**	1925	**Manna**
1903	**Rock Sand**	1926	**Colorado**
1904	**St Amant**	1927	**Adam's Apple**
1905	**Vedas**	1928	**Flamingo**
1906	**Gorgos**	1929	**Mr Jinks**
1907	**Slieve Gallion**	1930	**Diolite**
1908	**Norman III**	1931	**Cameronian**
1909	**Minoru**	1932	**Orwell**
1910	**Neil Gow**	1933	**Rodosto**
1911	**Sunstar**	1934	**Colombo**
1912	**Sweeper II**	1935	**Bahram**
1913	**Louvois**	1936	**Pay Up**
1914	**Kennymore**	1937	**Le Ksar**
1915	**Pommern**	1938	**Pasch**
1916	**Clarissimus**	1939	**Blue Peter**
1917	**Gay Crusader**	1940	* **Diebel**
1918	**Gainsborough**	1941	* **Lambert Simnel**
1919	**The Panther**	1942	* **Big Game**
1920	**Tetratema**	1943	* **Kingsway**
1921	**Craig an Eran**	1944	* **Garden Path**
1922	**St Louis**	1945	* **Court Martial**

		Trainer	Jockey	SP
1946	**Happy Knight**	H Jelliss	T Weston	28-1
1947	**Tudor Minstrel**	F Darling	G Richards	11-8
1948	**My Babu**	F Armstrong	C Smirke	2-1
1949	**Nimbus**	G Colling	EC Elliott	10-1
1950	**Palestine**	M Marsh	C Smirke	4-1
1951	**Ki Ming**	M Beary	A Breasley	100-8
1952	**Thunderhead II**	E Pollet	R Poincelet	100-7
1953	**Nearula**	C Elsey	E Britt	2-1
1954	**Darius**	H Wragg	E Mercer	8-1
1955	**Our Babu**	G Brooke	D Smith	13-2
1956	**Gilles de Retz**	C Jerdein	F Barlow	50-1
1957	**Crepello**	N Murless	L Piggott	7-2
1958	**Pall Mall**	C B-Rochfort	D Smith	20-1
1959	**Taboun**	A Head	G Moore	5-2
1960	**Martial**	PJ Prendergast	R Hutchinson	18-1
1961	**Rockavon**	G Boyd	N Stirk	66-1
1962	**Privy Councillor**	T Waugh	W Rickaby	100-6
1963	**Only For Life**	J Tree	J Lindley	33-1
1964	**Baldric II**	E Fellows	W Pyers	20-1
1965	**Niksar**	W Nightingall	D Keith	100-8
1966	**Kashmir II**	C Bartholomew	J Lindley	7-1
1967	**Royal Palace**	N Murless	G Moore	100-30
1968	**Sir Ivor**	MV O'Brien	L Piggott	11-8
1969	**Right Tack**	J Sutcliffe Jr	G Lewis	15-2
1970	**Nijinsky**	MV O'Brien	L Piggott	4-7
1971	**Brigadier Gerard**	W Hern	J Mercer	11-2

1972	**High Top**	B van Cutsem	W Carson	85-40
1973	**Mon Fils**	R Hannon	F Durr	50-1
1974	**Nonoalco**	F Boutin	Y Saint-Martin	19-2
1975	**Bolkonski**	H Cecil	G Dettori	33-1
1976	**Wollow**	H Cecil	G Dettori	Evens
1977	**Nebbiolo**	K Prendergast	G Curran	20-1
1978	**Roland Gardens**	D Sasse	F Durr	28-1
1979	**Tap On Wood**	B Hills	S Cauthen	20-1
1980	**Known Fact**	J Tree	W Carson	14-1
1981	**To-Agori-Mou**	G Harwood	G Starkey	5-2
1982	**Zino**	F Boutin	F Head	8-1
1983	**Lomond**	MV O'Brien	P Eddery	9-1

THE OAKS

Epsom 1½m 3-y-o f

* Run at Newmarket.

1779	**Bridget**	1811	**Sorcery**
1780	**Teetotum**	1812	**Manuella**
1781	**Faith**	1813	**Music**
1782	**Ceres**	1814	**Medora**
1783	**Maid of the Oaks**	1815	**Minuet**
1784	**Stella**	1816	**Landscape**
1785	**Trifle**	1817	**Neva**
1786	**The Yellow Filly**	1818	**Corinne**
1787	**Annette**	1819	**Shoveler**
1788	**Nightshade**	1820	**Caroline**
1789	**Tag**	1821	**Augusta**
1790	**Hippolyta**	1822	**Pastille**
1791	**Portia**	1823	**Zinc**
1792	**Volante**	1824	**Cobweb**
1793	**Coelia**	1825	**Wings**
1794	**Hermione**	1826	**Lilias (re-named Babel)**
1795	**Platina**	1827	**Gulnare**
1796	**Parisot**	1828	**Turquoise**
1797	**Nike**	1829	**Green Mantle**
1798	**Bellissima**	1830	**Variation**
1799	**Bellina**	1831	**Oxygen**
1800	**Ephemera**	1832	**Galata**
1801	**Eleanor**	1833	**Vespa**
1802	**Scotia**	1834	**Pussy**
1803	**Theophania**	1835	**Queen of Trumps**
1804	**Pelisse**	1836	**Cyprian**
1805	**Meteora**	1837	**Miss Letty**
1806	**Bronze**	1838	**Industry**
1807	**Briseis**	1839	**Deception**
1808	**Morel**	1840	**Crucifix**
1809	**Maid of Orleans**	1841	**Ghuznee**
1810	**Oriana**	1842	**Our Nell**

1843	Poison	1894	Amiable
1844	The Princess	1895	La Sagesse
1845	Refraction	1896	Canterbury Pilgrim
1846	Mendicant	1897	Limasol
1847	Miami	1898	Airs and Graces
1848	Cymba	1899	Musa
1849	Lady Evelyn	1900	La Roche
1850	Rhedycina	1901	Cap and Bells II
1851	Iris	1902	Sceptre
1852	Songstress	1903	Our Lassie
1853	Catherine Hayes	1904	Pretty Polly
1854	Mincemeat	1905	Cherry Lass
1855	Marchioness	1906	Keystone II
1856	Mincepie	1907	Glass Doll
1857	Blink Bonny	1908	Signorinetta
1858	Governess	1909	Perola
1859	Summerside	1910	Rosedrop
1860	Butterfly	1911	Cherimoya
1861	Brown Duchess	1912	Mirska
1862	Feu de Joie	1913	Jest
1863	Queen Bertha	1914	Princess Dorrie
1864	Fille de l'Air	1915 *	Snow Marten
1865	Regalia	1916 *	Fifinella
1866	Tormentor	1917 *	Sunny Jane
1867	Hippia	1918 *	My Dear
1868	Formosa	1919	Bayuda
1869	Brigantine	1920	Charlebelle
1870	Gamos	1921	Love in Idleness
1871	Hannah	1922	Pogrom
1872	Reine	1923	Brownhylda
1873	Marie Stuart	1924	Straitlace
1874	Apology	1925	Saucy Sue
1875	Spinaway	1926	Short Story
1876	Enguerrande	1927	Beam
	Camelia	1928	Toboggan
1877	Placida	1929	Pennycomequick
1878	Jannette	1930	Rose of England
1879	Wheel of Fortune	1931	Brulette
1880	Jenny Howlet	1932	Udaipur
1881	Thebais	1933	Chatelaine
1882	Geheimniss	1934	Light Brocade
1883	Bonny Jean	1935	Quashed
1884	Busybody	1936	Lovely Rosa
1885	Lonely	1937	Exhibitionnist
1886	Miss Jummy	1938	Rockfel
1887	Reve d'Or	1939	Galatea II
1888	Seabreeze	1940 *	Godiva
1889	L'Abbesse de Jouarre	1941 *	Commotion
1890	Memoir	1942 *	Sun Chariot
1891	Mimi	1943 *	Why Hurry
1892	La Fleche	1944 *	Hycilla
1893	Mrs Butterwick	1945 *	Sun Stream

	Trainer	Jockey	SP
1946 **Steady Aim**	F Butters	H Wragg	7-1
1947 **Imprudence**	J Lieux	W Johnstone	7-4
1948 **Masaka**	F Butters	W Nevett	7-1
1949 **Musidora**	C Elsey	E Britt	4-1
1950 **Asmena**	C Semblat	W Johnstone	5-1
1951 **Neasham Belle**	G Brooke	S Clayton	33-1
1952 **Frieze**	C Elsey	E Britt	100-7
1953 **Ambiguity**	RJ Colling	J Mercer	18-1
1954 **Sun Cap**	R Carver	W Johnstone	100-8
1955 **Meld**	C B-Rochfort	W Carr	7-4
1956 **Sicarelle**	F Mathet	F Palmer	3-1
1957 **Carrozza**	N Murless	L Piggott	100-8
1958 **Bella Paola**	F Mathet	M Garcia	6-4
1959 **Petite Etoile**	N Murless	L Piggott	11-2
1960 **Never Too Late**	E Pollet	R Poincelet	6-5
1961 **Sweet Solera**	F Day	W Rickaby	11-4
1962 **Monade**	J Lieux	Y Saint-Martin	7-1
1963 **Noblesse**	PJ Prendergast	G Bougoure	4-11
1964 **Homeward Bound**	J Oxley	G Starkey	100-7
1965 **Long Look**	MV O'Brien	J Purtell	100-7
1966 **Valoris**	MV O'Brien	L Piggott	11-10
1967 **Pia**	W Elsey	E Hide	100-7
1968 **La Lagune**	F Boutin	G Thiboeuf	11-8
1969 **Sleeping Partner**	Doug Smith	J Gorton	100-6
1970 **Lupe**	N Murless	A Barclay	100-30
1971 **Altesse Royale**	N Murless	G Lewis	6-4
1972 **Ginevra**	Ryan Price	A Murray	8-1
1973 **Mysterious**	N Murless	G Lewis	13-8
1974 **Polygamy**	P Walwyn	P Eddery	3-1
1975 **Julliette Marny**	J Tree	L Piggott	12-1
1976 **Pawneese**	A Penna	Y Saint-Martin	6-5
1977 **Dunfermline**	W Hern	W Carson	6-1
1978 **Fair Salinia**	M Stoute	G Starkey	8-1
1979 **Scintillate**	J Tree	P Eddery	20-1
1980 **Bireme**	W Hern	W Carson	9-2
1981 **Blue Wind**	D Weld	L Piggott	3-1
1982 **Time Charter**	H Candy	W Newnes	12-1
1983 **Sun Princess**	W Hern	W Carson	6-1

THE ST LEGER

Doncaster 1¾m 127y 3-y-o

1776	**Allabaculla**	1780	**Ruler**
1777	**Bourbon**	1781	**Serina**
1778	**Hollandaise**	1782	**Imperatrix**
1779	**Tommy**	1783	**Phenomenon**

1784	Omphale	1836	Elis
1785	Cowslip	1837	Mango
1786	Paragon	1838	Don John
1787	Spadille	1839	Charles XII
1788	Young Flora	1840	Launcelot
1789	Pewett	1841	Satirist
1790	Ambidexter	1842	Blue Bonnet
1791	Y Traveller	1843	Nutwith
1792	Tartar	1844	Faugh-a-Ballagh
1793	Ninety-three	1845	The Baron
1794	Beningbrough	1846	Sir Tatton Sykes
1795	Hambletonian	1847	Van Tromp
1796	Ambrosio	1848	Surplice
1797	Lounger	1849	The Flying Dutchman
1798	Symmetry	1850	Voltigeur
1799	Cockfighter	1851	Newminster
1800	Champion	1852	Stockwell
1801	Quiz	1853	West Australian
1802	Orville	1854	Knight of St George
1803	Remembrancer	1855	Saucebox
1804	Sancho	1856	Warlock
1805	Staveley	1857	Imperieuse
1806	Fyldener	1858	Sunbeam
1807	Paulina	1859	Gamester
1808	Petronius	1860	St Albans
1809	Ashton	1861	Caller Ou
1810	Octasvian	1862	The Marquis
1811	Soothsayer	1863	Lord Clifden
1812	Otterington	1864	Blair Athol
1813	Altisidora	1865	Gladiateur
1814	William	1866	Lord Lyon
1815	Filho da Puta	1867	Achievement
1816	The Duchess	1868	Formosa
1817	Ebor	1869	Pero Gomez
1818	Reveller	1870	Hawthornden
1819	Antonio	1871	Hannah
1820	St Patrick	1872	Wenlock
1821	Jack Spigot	1873	Marie Stuart
1822	Theodore	1874	Apology
1823	Barefoot	1875	Craig Millar
1824	Jerry	1876	Petrarch
1825	Memnon	1877	Silvio
1826	Tarrare	1878	Jannette
1827	Matilda	1879	Rayon d'Or
1828	The Colonel	1880	Robert the Devil
1829	Rowton	1881	Iroquois
1830	Birmingham	1882	Dutch Oven
1831	Chorister	1883	Ossian
1832	Margrave	1884	The Lambkin
1833	Rockingham	1885	Melton
1834	Touchstone	1886	Ormonde
1835	Queen of Trumps	1887	Kilwarlin

1888	Seabreeze	1917	Gay Crusader
1889	Donovan	1918	Gainsborough
1890	Memoir	1919	Keysoe
1891	Common	1920	Caligula
1892	La Fleche	1921	Polemarch
1893	Isinglass	1922	Royal Lancer
1894	Throstle	1923	Tranquil
1895	Sir Visto	1924	Salmon-Trout
1896	Persimmon	1925	Solario
1897	Galtee More	1926	Coronach
1898	Wildfowler	1927	Book Law
1899	Flying Fox	1928	Fairway
1900	Diamond Jubilee	1929	Trigo
1901	Doricles	1930	Singapore
1902	Sceptre	1931	Sandwich
1903	Rock Sand	1932	Firdaussi
1904	Pretty Polly	1933	Hyperion
1905	Challacombe	1934	Windsor Lad
1906	Troutbeck	1935	Bahram
1907	Wool Winder	1936	Boswell
1908	Your Majesty	1937	Chulmleigh
1909	Bayardo	1938	Scottish Union
1910	Swynford	1939	No race
1911	Prince Palatine	1940	Turkhan
1912	Tracery	1941	Sun Castle
1913	Night Hawk	1942	Sun Chariot
1914	Black Jester	1943	Herringbone
1915	Pommern	1944	Tehran
1916	Hurry On	1945	Chamossaire

		Trainer	Jockey	SP
1946	Airborne	R Perryman	T Lowrey	3-1
1947	Sayajirao	F Armstrong	E Britt	9-2
1948	Black Tarquin	C B-Rochfort	E Britt	15-2
1949	Ridge Wood	N Murless	M Beary	100-7
1950	Scratch II	C Semblat	W Johnstone	9-2
1951	Talma II	C Semblat	W Johnstone	7-1
1952	Tulyar	M Marsh	C Smirke	10-11
1953	Premonition	C B-Rochfort	E Smith	10-1
1954	Never Say Die	J Lawson	C Smirke	100-30
1955	Meld	C B-Rochfort	W Carr	10-11
1956	Cambremer	C Bridgland	F Palmer	8-1
1957	Ballymoss	MV O'Brien	TP Burns	8-1
1958	Alcide	C B-Rochfort	W Carr	4-9
1959	Cantelo	C Elsey	E Hide	100-7
1960	St Paddy	N Murless	L Piggott	4-6
1961	Aurelius	N Murless	L Piggott	9-2
1962	Hethersett	W Hern	W Carr	100-8
1963	Ragusa	PJ Prendergast	G Bougoure	2-5
1964	Indiana	JF Watts	J Lindley	100-7
1965	Provoke	W Hern	J Mercer	28-1

1966	**Sodium**	G Todd	F Durr	7-1
1967	**Ribocco**	R Johnson Houghton	L Piggott	7-2
1968	**Ribero**	R Johnson Houghton	L Piggott	100-30
1969	**Intermezzo**	H Wragg	R Hutchinson	7-1
1970	**Nijinsky**	MV O'Brien	L Piggott	2-7
1971	**Athens Wood**	H Thomson Jones	L Piggott	5-2
1972	**Boucher**	MV O'Brien	L Piggott	3-1
1973	**Peleid**	W Elsey	F Durr	28-1
1974	**Bustino**	W Hern	J Mercer	11-10
1975	**Bruni**	Ryan Price	A Murray	9-1
1976	**Crow**	A Penna	Y Saint-Martin	6-1
1977	**Dunfermline**	W Hern	W Carson	10-1
1978	**Julio Mariner**	B Brittain	E Hide	28-1
1979	**Son Of Love**	R Collett	A Lequeux	20-1
1980	**Light Cavalry**	H Cecil	J Mercer	3-1
1981	**Cut Above**	W Hern	J Mercer	28-1
1982	**Touching Wood**	H Thomson Jones	P Cook	7-1
1983	**Sun Princess**	W Hern	W Carson	11-8

Run at Newmarket as the September Stakes in 1915-18, at
Thirsk as the Yorkshire St Leger in 1940, at Manchester as New
St Leger in 1941, at Newmarket as New St Leger in 1942-4 and
at York in 1945. Run over 2 miles up to 1812 and over 1 mile
6 f 193 yds from 1813 to 1825 and over 1 mile 6 f 132 yds
from 1826 to 1969.

Secretariat, winner of the American Triple Crown in 1973

AMERICAN TRIPLE CROWN

Kentucky Derby (1¼ miles, Churchill Downs, Louisville, Kentucky). First run in 1875.
Preakness Stakes (1 mile 1½ fur, Pimlico, Baltimore, Maryland). First run in 1873.
Belmont Stakes (1½ miles, Belmont Park, Long Island, New York). First run in 1867.

	Kentucky Derby	**Preakness**	**Belmont**
1920	Paul Jones	Man o'War	Man o'War
1921	Behave Yourself	Broomspun	Grey Lag
1922	Morvich	Pillory	Pillory
1923	Zev	Vigil	Zev
1924	Black Gold	Nellie Morse	Mad Play
1925	Flying Ebony	Coventry	American Flag
1926	Bubbling Over	Display	Crusader
1927	Whiskery	Bostonian	Chance Shot
1928	Reigh Count	Victorian	Vito
1929	Clyde van Dusen	Dr Freeland	Blue Larkspur
1930	* Gallant Fox	Gallant Fox	Gallant Fox
1931	Twenty Grand	Mate	Twenty Grand
1932	Burgoo King	Burgoo King	Faireno
1933	Brokers Tip	Head Play	Hurry Off
1934	Cavalcade	High Quest	Peace Chance
1935	* Omaha	Omaha	Omaha
1936	Bold Venture	Bold Venture	Granville
1937	* War Admiral	War Admiral	War Admiral
1938	Lawrin	Dauber	Pasteurized
1939	Johnstown	Challedon	Johnstown
1940	Gallahadion	Bimelech	Bimelech
1941	* Whirlaway	Whirlaway	Whirlaway
1942	Shut Out	Alsab	Shut Out
1943	* Count Fleet	Count Fleet	Count Fleet
1944	Pensive	Pensive	Bounding Home
1945	Hoop Jr	Polynesian	Pavot
1946	* Assault	Assault	Assault
1947	Jet Pilot	Faultless	Phalanx
1948	* Citation	Citation	Citation
1949	Ponder	Capot	Capot
1950	Middleground	Hill Prince	Middleground
1951	Count Turf	Bold	Counterpoint
1952	Hill Gail	Blue Man	One Count
1953	Dark Star	Native Dancer	Native Dancer
1954	Determine	Hasty Road	High Gun
1955	Swaps	Nashua	Nashua
1956	Needles	Fabius	Needles
1957	Iron Liege	Bold Ruler	Gallant Man
1958	Tim Tam	Tim Tam	Cavan
1959	Tomy Lee	Royal Orbit	Sword Dancer
1960	Venetian Way	Bally Ache	Celtic Ash

1961	Carry Back	Carry Back	Sherluck
1962	Decidedly	Greek Money	Jaipur
1963	Chateaugay	Candy Spots	Chateaugay
1964	Northern Dancer	Northern Dancer	Quadrangle
1965	Lucky Debonair	Tom Rolfe	Hail to All
1966	Kauai King	Kauai King	Amberoid
1967	Proud Clarion	Damascus	Damascus
1968	Dancers Image	Forward Pass	Stage Door Johnny
1969	Majestic Prince	Majestic Prince	Arts and Letters
1970	Dust Commander	Personality	High Echelon
1971	Canonero II	Canonero II	Pass Catcher
1972	Riva Ridge	Bee Bee Bee	Riva Ridge
1973	* Secretariat	Secretariat	Secretariat
1974	Cannonade	Little Current	Little Current
1975	Foolish Pleasure	Master Derby	Avatar
1976	Bold Forbes	Elocutionist	Bold Forbes
1977	* Seattle Slew	Seattle Slew	Seattle Slew
1978	* Affirmed	Affirmed	Affirmed
1979	Spectacular Bid	Spectacular Bid	Coastal
1980	Genuine Risk	Codex	Temperance Hill
1981	Pleasant Colony	Pleasant Colony	Summing
1982	Gato Del Sol	Alamo's Ruler	Conquistador Cielo
1983	Sunny's Halo	Deputed Testamony	Caveat

* Triple Crown winner

OTHER IMPORTANT RACES

(In the order in which they take place in the Racing calendar)

GOLD CUP

Royal Ascot 2½m

		Trainer	Jockey	SP
1946	**Caracalla II**	C Semblat	C Elliott	4-9
1947	**Souverain**	H Delavaud	M Lollieron	6-4
1948	**Arbar**	C Semblat	C Elliott	4-6
1949	**Alycidon**	W Earl	D Smith	5-4
1950	**Supertello**	JC Waugh	D Smith	10-1
1951	**Pan II**	E Pollet	R Poincelet	100-8
1952	**Aquino II**	F Armstrong	G Richards	4-1
1953	**Souepi**	G Digby	C Elliott	11-2
1954	**Elpenor**	C Elliott	J Doyasbere	100-8
1955	**Botticelli**	U Penco	E Camici	9-4
1956	**Macip**	C Elliott	S Boullenger	6-1
1957	**Zarathustra**	C B-Rochfort	L Piggott	6-1
1958	**Gladness**	MV O'Brien	L Piggott	3-1
1959	**Wallaby II**	P Carter	F Palmer	9-4

		Trainer	Jockey	SP
1960	**Sheshoon**	A Head	G Moore	7-4
1961	**Pandofell**	F Maxwell	L Piggott	100-8
1962	**Balto**	M Bonaventure	F Palmer	7-4
1963	**Twilight Alley**	N Murless	L Piggott	100-30
1964	No Race			
1965	**Fighting Charlie**	F Maxwell	L Piggott	6-1
1966	**Fighting Charlie**	F Maxwell	G Starkey	15-8
1967	**Parbury**	D Candy	J Mercer	7-1
1968	**Pardallo II**	C Bartholomew	W Pyers	13-2
1969	**Levmoss**	S McGrath	W Williamson	15-8
1970	**Preicipice Wood**	Mrs R Lomax	J Lindley	5-1
1971	**Random Shot**	A Budgett	G Lewis	11-1
1972	**Erimo Hawk**	G Barling	P Eddery	10-1
1973	**Lassalle**	R Carver	J Lindley	2-1
1974	**Ragstone**	J Dunlop	R Hutchinson	6-4
1975	**Sagaro**	F Boutin	L Piggott	7-4
1976	**Sagaro**	F Boutin	L Piggott	8-15
1977	**Sagaro**	F Boutin	L Piggott	9-4
1978	**Shangamuzo**	M Stoute	G Starkey	13-2
1979	**Le Moss**	H Cecil	L Piggott	7-4
1980	**Le Moss**	H Cecil	J Mercer	3-1
1981	**Ardross**	H Cecil	L Piggott	30-100
1982	**Ar dross**	H Cecil	L Piggott	1-5
1983	**Little Wolf**	W Hern	W Carson	4-1

First run in 1807. Run as Emperor's Plate 1845-53.

CORAL ECLIPSE STAKES

Sandown 1¼ m

		Trainer	Jockey	SP
1946	**Gulf Stream**	W Earl	H Wragg	8-13
1947	**Migoli**	F Butters	C Smirke	7-2
1948	**Petition**	F Butters	K Gethin	8-1
1949	**Djeddah**	C Semblat	C Elliott	6-4
1950	**Flocon**	P Carter	F Palmer	100-9
1951	**Mystery IX**	P Carter	L Piggott	100-8
1952	**Tulyar**	M Marsh	C Smirke	1-3
1953	**Argur**	J Glynn	C Elliott	100-9
1954	**King Of The Tudors**	W Stephenson	K Gethin	9-2
1955	**Darius**	H Wragg	L Piggott	11-10
1956	**Tropique**	G Watson	P Blanc	3-1
1957	**Arctic Explorer**	N Murless	L Piggott	100-30
1958	**Ballymoss**	MV O'Brien	A Breasley	8-11
1959	**Saint Crespin III**	A Head	G Moore	5-2
1960	**Javelot**	P Carter	F Palmer	4-1
1961	**St Paddy**	N Murless	L Piggott	2-13

1962	**Henry The Seventh**	W Elsey	E Hide	8-11
1963	**Khalkis**	PJ Prendergast	G Bougoure	7-4
1964	**Ragusa**	PJ Prendergast	G Bougoure	4-6
1965	**Canisbay**	C B-Rochfort	S Clayton	20-1
1966	**Pieces Of Eight**	MV O'Brien	L Piggott	15-2
1967	**Busted**	N Murless	W Rickaby	8-1
1968	**Royal Palace**	N Murless	A Barclay	9-4
1969	**Wolver Hollow**	H Cecil	L Piggott	8-1
1970	**Connaught**	N Murless	A Barclay	5-4
1971	**Mill Reef**	I Balding	G Lewis	5-4
1972	**Brigadier Gerard**	W Hern	J Mercer	4-11
1973	**Scottish Rifle**	J Dunlop	R Hutchinson	15-8
1974	**Coup de Feu**	D Sasse	P Eddery	33-1
1975	**Star Appeal**	T Greiper	G Starkey	20-1
1976	**Wollow**	H Cecil	G Dettori	9-4
1977	**Artaius**	MV O'Brien	L Piggott	9-2
1978	**Gunner B**	H Cecil	J Mercer	7-4
1979	**Dickens Hill**	M O'Toole	A Murray	7-4
1980	**Ela-Mana-Mou**	W Hern	W Carson	85-40
1981	**Master Willie**	H Candy	P Waldron	6-4
1982	**Kalaglow**	G Harwood	G Starkey	11-10
1983	**Solford**	MV O'Brien	P Eddery	3-1

Run from 1886 to 1973 as Eclipse Stakes and
in 1974-75 as Benson and Hedges Eclipse Stakes.

WILLIAM HILL JULY CUP

Newmarket 6f

		Trainer	Jockey	SP
1946	**The Bug**	H Wellesley	C Smirke	8-11
1947	**Falls Of Clyde**	E Williams	S Wragg	100-30
1948	**Palm Vista**	P Beasley	E Smith	13-8
1949	**Abernant**	N Murless	G Richards	2-11
1950	**Abernant**	N Murless	G Richards	8-13
1951	**Hard Sauce**	N Bertie	G Richards	8-1
1952	**Set Fair**	W Nightingall	E Smith	15-8
1953	**Devon Vintage**	R Colling	G Richards	11-4
1954	**Vilmoray**	B Bullock	W Snaith	6-4
1955	**Pappa Fourway**	W Dutton	W Carr	1-6
1956	**Matador**	JA Waugh	W Rickaby	11-2
1957	**Vigo**	W Dutton	L Piggott	7-2
1958	**Right Boy**	W Dutton	L Piggott	4-5
1959	**Right Boy**	H Rohan	L Piggott	11-10
1960	**Tin Whistle**	H Rohan	L Piggott	WO
1961	**Galivanter**	W Hern	W Carr	9-2
1962	**Marsolve**	R Day	W Rickaby	5-1

1963	**Secret Step**	P H-Bass	G Lewis	2-1
1964	**Daylight Robbery**	A Budgett	A Breasley	100-9
1965	**Merry Madcap**	F Maxwell	R Hutchinson	100-8
1966	**Lucasland**	JA Waugh	E Eldin	100-6
1967	**Forlorn River**	WA Stephenson	B Raymond	8-1
1968	**So Blessed**	M Jarvis	F Durr	7-2
1969	**Tudor Music**	M Jarvis	F Durr	4-5
1970	**Huntercombe**	A Budgett	A Barclay	8-13
1971	**Realm**	J Winter	B Taylor	11-2
1972	**Parsimony**	R Johnson Houghton	R Hutchinson	16-1
1973	**Thatch**	MV O'Brien	L Piggott	4-5
1974	**Saritamer**	MV O'Brien	L Piggott	11-4
1975	**Lianga**	A Penna	Y Saint-Martin	10-1
1976	**Lochnager**	MW Easterby	E Hide	3-1
1977	**Gentilhombre**	N Adam	P Cook	10-1
1978	**Solinus**	MV O'Brien	L Piggott	4-7
1979	**Thatching**	MV O'Brien	L Piggott	2-1
1980	**Moorestyle**	R Armstrong	L Piggott	3-1
1981	**Marwell**	M Stoute	WR Swinburn	13-8
1982	**Sharpo**	J Tree	P Eddery	13-2
1983	**Habibti**	J Dunlop	W Carson	8-1

First run as July Cup in 1876. Renamed in 1978.

KING GEORGE VI AND QUEEN ELIZABETH DIAMOND STAKES

Ascot 1½m

		Trainer	Jockey	SP
1951	**Supreme Court**	E Williams	C Elliott	100-9
1952	**Tulyar**	M Marsh	C Smirke	3-1
1953	**Pinza**	N Bertie	G Richards	2-1
1954	**Aureole**	C B-Rochfort	E Smith	9-2
1955	**Vimy**	A Head	R Poincelet	10-1
1956	**Ribot**	U Penco	E Camici	2-5
1957	**Montaval**	G Bridgland	F Palmer	20-1
1958	**Ballymoss**	MV O'Brien	A Breasley	7-4
1959	**Alcide**	C B-Rochfort	W Carr	2-1
1960	**Aggressor**	J Gosden	J Lindley	100-8
1961	**Right Royal V**	E Pollet	R Poincelet	6-4
1962	**Match III**	F Mathet	Y Saint-Martin	9-2
1963	**Ragusa**	PJ Prendergast	G Bougoure	4-1
1964	**Nasram II**	E Fellows	W Pyers	100-7
1965	**Meadow Court**	PJ Prendergast	L Piggott	6-5
1966	**Aunt Edith**	N Murless	L Piggott	7-2
1967	**Busted**	N Murless	G Moore	4-1
1968	**Royal Palace**	N Murless	A Barclay	7-4
1969	**Park Top**	B van Cutsem	L Piggott	9-4

Year	Horse	Trainer	Jockey	SP
1970	**Nijinsky**	MV O'Brien	L Piggott	40-85
1971	**Mill Reef**	I Balding	G Lewis	8-13
1972	**Brigadier Gerard**	W Hern	J Mercer	8-13
1973	**Dahlia**	M Zilber	W Pyers	10-1
1974	**Dahlia**	M Zilber	L Piggott	15-8
1975	**Grundy**	P Walwyn	P Eddery	4-5
1976	**Pawneese**	A Penna	Y Saint-Martin	9-4
1977	**The Minstrel**	MV O'Brien	L Piggott	7-4
1978	**Ile de Bourbon**	R Johnson Houghton	J Reid	12-1
1979	**Troy**	W Hern	W Carson	2-5
1980	**Ela-Mana-Mou**	W Hern	W Carson	11-4
1981	**Shergar**	M Stoute	WR Swinburn	2-5
1982	**Kalaglow**	G Harwood	G Starkey	13-2
1983	**Time Charter**	H Candy	J Mercer	5-1

Run as King George VI and Queen Elizabeth Stakes from 1952-74.

SUSSEX STAKES

Goodwood 1m

Year	Horse	Trainer	Jockey	SP
1946	**Radiotherapy**	F Templeman	G Richards	7-4
1947	**Combat**	F Darling	G Richards	8-13
1948	**My Babu**	F Armstrong	C Smirke	1-3
1949	**Krakatao**	N Murless	G Richards	2-11
1950	**Palestine**	M Marsh	C Smirke	1-2
1951	**Le Sage**	T Carey	G Richards	6-4
1952	**Agitator**	N Murless	G Richards	8-13
1953	**King Of The Tudors**	W Stephenson	C Spares	11-10
1954	**Landau**	N Murless	W Snaith	6-4
1955	**My Kingdom**	W Nightingall	D Smith	13-2
1956	**Lucero**	H Wragg	E Mercer	8-1
1957	**Quorum**	W Lyde	A Russell	10-11
1958	**Major Portion**	T Leader	E Smith	8-11
1959	**Petite Etoile**	N Murless	L Piggott	1-10
1960	**Venture VII**	A Head	G Moore	8-13
1961	**Le Levanstell**	S McGrath	W Williamson	100-7
1962	**Romulus**	R Johnson Houghton	W Swinburn	9-1
1963	**Queen's Hussar**	T Corbett	R Hutchinson	25-1
1964	**Roan Rocket**	G Todd	L Piggott	4-6
1965	**Carlemont**	PJ Prendergast	R Hutchinson	7-2
1966	**Paveh**	T Ainsworth	R Hutchinson	5-1
1967	**Reform**	Sir G Richards	A Breasley	Evens
1968	**Petingo**	F Armstrong	L Piggott	6-4
1969	**Jimmy Peppin**	J Sutcliffe Jr	G Lewis	7-4

1970	**Humble Duty**	P Walwyn	D Keith	11-8
1971	**Brigadier Gerard**	W Hern	J Mercer	4-6
1972	**Sallust**	W Hern	J Mercer	9-2
1973	**Thatch**	MV O'Brien	L Piggott	4-5
1974	**Ace of Aces**	M Zilber	J Lindley	8-1
1975	**Bolkonski**	H Cecil	C Dettori	1-2
1976	**Wollow**	H Cecil	G Dettori	10-11
1977	**Artaius**	MV O'Brien	L Piggott	6-4
1978	**Jaazeiro**	MV O'Brien	L Piggott	8-13
1979	**Kris**	H Cecil	J Mercer	4-5
1980	**Posse**	J Dunlop	P Eddery	8-13
1981	**King's Lake**	MV O'Brien	P Eddery	5-2
1982	**On The House**	H Wragg	J Reid	14-1
1983	**Noalcoholic**	G Pritchard-Gordon	G Duffield	18-1

First run in 1841. From 1900-59 the race was for
three-year-olds only. From 1960 for three and four-year-olds only.

GOODWOOD CUP

Goodwood 2m 5f

		Trainer	Jockey	SP
1946	**Marsyas II**	C Semblat	C Elliott	1-3
1947	**Monsieur L'Amiral**	E Charlier	C Smirke	1-2
1948	**Tenerani**	N Bertie	E Camici	100-30
1949	**Alycidon**	W Earl	D Smith	30-100
1950	**Val Drake**	R Carver	R Poincelet	4-1
1951	**Pan II**	E Pollet	R Poincelet	5-6
1952	**Medway**	F Winter	D Smith	5-1
1953	**Souepi**	G Digby	C Elliott	2-1
1954	**Blarney Stone**	V Smyth	W Rickaby	13-2
1955	**Double Bore**	J Tree	T Gosling	9-1
1956	**Zarathustra**	C B-Rochfort	W Carr	10-11
1957	**Tenterhooks**	C Elsey	E Britt	2-1
1958	**Gladness**	MV O'Brien	L Piggott	1-2
1959	**Dickens**	C B-Rochfort	D Smith	9-4
1960	**Exar**	N Murless	L Piggott	4-9
1961	**Predominate**	T Leader	E Smith	11-4
1962	**Sagacity**	C B-Rochfort	W Carr	5-1
1963	**Trelawny**	G Todd	A Breasley	8-13
1964	**Raise You Ten**	C B-Rochfort	S Clayton	Evens
1965	**Apprentice**	C B-Rochfort	S Clayton	8-1
1966	**Gaulois**	C B-Rochfort	R Hutchinson	15-2
1967	**Wrekin Rambler**	Sir G Richards	A Breasley	2-1
1968	**Ovaltine**	J Watts	B Taylor	5-2
1969	**Richmond Fair**	B Hobbs	J Gorton	5-4
1970	**Parthenon**	H Cecil	G Starkey	3-1

1971	**Rock Roi**	P Walwyn	D Keith	4-6
1972	**Erimo Hawk**	G Barling	P Eddery	10-11
1973	**Proverb**	B Hills	E Johnson	6-4
1974	**Proverb**	B Hills	L Piggott	4-5
1975	**Girandole**	M Stoute	L Piggott	7-2
1976	**Mr Bigmore**	P Robinson	G Starkey	3-1
1977	**Grey Baron**	B Hobbs	G Lewis	11-4
1978	**Tug Of War**	D Whelan	B Rouse	20-1
1979	**Le Moss**	H Cecil	J Mercer	1-2
1980	**Le Moss**	H Cecil	J Mercer	4-7
1981	**Ardross**	H Cecil	L Piggott	2-9
1982	**Heighlin**	D Elsworth	S Cauthen	8-1
1983	**Little Wolf**	W Hern	W Carson	4-9

First run in 1812.

BENSON AND HEDGES GOLD CUP

York 1m 2½f

		Trainer	Jockey	SP
1972	**Roberto**	MV O'Brien	B Baeza	12-1
1973	**Moulton**	H Wragg	G Lewis	14-1
1974	**Dahlia**	M Zilber	L Piggott	8-15
1975	**Dahlia**	M Zilber	L Piggott	7-2
1976	**Wollow**	H Cecil	G Dettori	9-4
1977	**Relkino**	W Hern	W Carson	33-1
1978	**Hawaiian Sound**	B Hills	L Piggott	2-1
1979	**Troy**	W Hern	W Carson	1-2
1980	**Master Willie**	H Candy	P Waldron	13-2
1981	**Beldale Flutter**	M Jarvis	P Eddery	9-1
1982	**Assert**	D O'Brien	P Eddery	4-5
1983	**Caerleon**	MV O'Brien	P Eddery	100-30

TOTE-EBOR HANDICAP

York 1¾m

		Trainer	Jockey	SP
1946	**Foxtrot**	E Lambton	E Britt	3-1
1947	**Procne**	C Elsey	J Sime	8-1
1948	**Donino**	A Cooper	J Sime	100-7
1949	**Miraculous Atom**	S Hall	W Nevett	100-7
1950	**Cadzow Oak**	J Thwaites	J Thomson	100-8
1951	**Bob**	C Elsey	E Carter	8-1
1952	**Signification**	J Pearce	H Jones	10-1
1953	**Norooz**	M Marsh	R Fawdon	100-9

Year	Horse	Trainer	Jockey	SP
1954	**By Thunder**	F Armstrong	W Swinburn	7-1
1955	**Hyperion Kid**	H Wragg	P Robinson	100-8
1956	**Donald**	J Jarvis	D Smith	5-1
1957	**Morecambe**	S Hall	J Sime	100-8
1958	**Gladness**	MV O'Brien	L Piggott	5-1
1959	**Primera**	N Murless	L Piggott	6-1
1960	**Persian Road**	J Tree	G Moore	18-1
1961	**Die Hard**	MV O'Brien	L Piggott	11-2
1962	**Sostenuto**	W Elsey	Don Morris	9-1
1963	**Partholon**	T Shaw	J Sime	100-6
1964	**Proper Pride**	W Wharton	D Smith	28-1
1965	**Twelfth Man**	H Wragg	P Cook	6-1
1966	**Lomond**	R Jarvis	E Eldin	100-8
1967	**Ovaltine**	J Watts	E Johnson	100-8
1968	**Alignment**	W Elsey	E Johnson	9-1
1969	**Big Hat**	D Hanley	R Still	40-1
1970	**Tintagel II**	R Sturdy	L Piggott	6-1
1971	**Knotty Pine**	M Jarvis	F Durr	9-2
1972	**Crazy Rhythm**	S Ingham	F Durr	19-2
1973	**Bonne Noel**	PJ Prendergast	C Roche	4-1
1974	**Anji**	J Sutcliffe Jr	T McKeown	20-1
1975	**Dakota**	S Hall	A Barclay	7-1
1976	**Sir Montagu**	Ryan Price	W Carson	11-4
1977	**Move Off**	W Calvert	J Bleasdale	9-1
1978	**Totowah**	M Jarvis	P Cook	20-1
1979	**Sea Pigeon**	MH Easterby	JJ O'Neill	18-1
1980	**Shaftesbury**	M Stoute	G Starkey	12-1
1981	**Protection Racket**	J Hindley	M Birch	15-2
1982	**Another Sam**	R Hannon	B Rouse	16-1
1983	**Jupiter Island**	C Brittain	L Piggott	9-1

Run from 1843 as the Ebor Handicap, from 1967 as the
Johnnie Walker Ebor Handicap and from 1974-75 as
Terry's All Gold Ebor Handicap. Renamed in 1976.

WILLIAM HILL SPRINT CHAMPIONSHIP

York 5f

Year	Horse	Trainer	Jockey	SP
1976	**Lochnager**	MW Easterby	E Hide	4-5
1977	**Haveroid**	N Adam	E Hide	10-1
1978	**Solinus**	MV O'Brien	L Piggott	1-2
1979	**Ahonoora**	F Durr	G Starkey	3-1
1980	**Sharpo**	J Tree	P Eddery	3-1
1981	**Sharpo**	J Tree	P Eddery	14-1
1982	**Sharpo**	J Tree	S Cauthen	Evens
1983	**Habibti**	J Dunlop	W Carson	13-8

Run in 1922-75 as Nunthorpe Stakes.

DONCASTER CUP

Doncaster 2¼ m

		Trainer	Jockey	SP
1946	**Marsyas II**	C Semblat	C Elliott	1-7
1947	**Trimbush**	P Vasey	D Smith	10-1
1948	**Auralia**	R Day	D Smith	6-1
1949	**Alycidon**	W Earl	D Smith	2-7
1950	**Aldborough**	F Walwyn	D Smith	6-1
1951	**Fast Fox**	P Carter	F Palmer	3-1
1952	**Aquino II**	F Armstrong	G Richards	2-1
1953	**Souepi**	G Digby	C Elliott	5-1
	Nick La Rocca	J Colling	J Mercer	100-7
1954	**Osborne**	C B-Rochfort	W Carr	5-1
1955	**Entente Cordiale**	G Colling	D Smith	5-2
1956	**Atlas**	C B-Rochfort	W Carr	11-4
1957	**French Beige**	H Peacock	G Littlewood	5-1
1958	**Agreement**	C B-Rochfort	D Smith	25-1
1959	**Agreement**	C B-Rochfort	W Carr	11-4
1960	**Exar**	N Murless	L Piggott	6-100
1961	**Pandofell**	F Maxwell	L Piggott	9-4
1962	**Bonnard**	J Clayton	R Hutchinson	6-1
1963	**Raise You Ten**	C B-Rochfort	D Smith	5-1
1964	**Grey Of Falloden**	W Hern	J Mercer	8-1
1965	**Prince Hansel**	D Thom	D Yates	2-1
1966	**Piaco**	G Barling	M Thomas	11-8
1967	**Crozier**	P Walwyn	F Durr	20-1
1968	**The Accuser**	W Hern	J Mercer	2-1
1969	**Canterbury**	PJ Prendergast	W Williamson	100-30
1970	**Magna Carta**	I Balding	G Lewis	6-4

Doug Smith, four wins in a row in the Doncaster Cup from 1947 to 1950

1971	**Rock Roi**	P Walwyn	D Keith	4-11
1972	**Biskrah**	A Breasley	J Mercer	4-1
1973	**Attica Meli**	N Murless	G Lewis	4-11
1974	**Proverb**	B Hills	W Carson	1-2
1975	**Crash Course**	J Hindley	A Kimberley	4-7
1976	**Sea Anchor**	W Hern	J Mercer	2-5
1977	**Shangamuzo**	G Hunter	P Eddery	33-1
1978	**Buckskin**	H Cecil	J Mercer	5-2
1979	**Le Moss**	H Cecil	J Mercer	4-11
1980	**Le Moss**	H Cecil	J Mercer	4-6
1981	**Protection Racket**	J Hindley	J Lowe	8-11
1982	**Ardross**	H Cecil	L Piggott	2-9
1983	**Karadar**	M Stoute	WR Swinburn	2-1

First run in 1801.

WILLIAM HILL CHEVELEY PARK STAKES

Newmarket 6f 2-y-o f

		Trainer	Jockey	SP
1946	**Djerba**	C Semblat	C Elliott	9-2
1947	**Ash Blonde**	J Colling	P Evans	100-8
1948	**Pambidian**	W Nightingall	G Richards	100-6
1949	**Corejada**	C Semblat	C Elliott	9-4
1950	**Belle Of All**	N Bertie	G Richards	5-4
1951	**Zabara**	V Smyth	G Richards	10-11
1952	**Bebe Grande**	F Armstrong	G Richards	1-2
1953	**Sixpence**	PJ Prendergast	G Richards	4-1
1954	**Gloria Nicky**	N Bertie	A Breasley	10-1
1955	**Midget II**	A Head	R Poincelet	Evens
1956	**Sarcelle**	N Cannon	A Breasley	4-6
1957	**Rich and Rare**	J Jarvis	E Mercer	5-1
1958	**Lindsay**	R Peacock	E Mercer	100-8
1959	**Queensbury**	JA Waugh	E Smith	2-5
1960	**Opaline II**	A Head	G Moore	11-10
1961	**Display**	PJ Prendergast	R Hutchinson	8-11
1962	**My Goodness Me**	G Brooke	E Smith	100-8
1963	**Crimea II**	C B-Rochfort	W Carr	9-1
1964	**Night Off**	W Wharton	J Mercer	20-1
1965	**Berkeley Springs**	I Balding	G Lewis	100-8
1966	**Fleet**	N Murless	L Piggott	5-2
1967	**Lalibela**	MV O'Brien	L Piggott	5-1
1968	**Mige**	A Head	J Taillard	5-2
1969	**Humble Duty**	P Walwyn	D Keith	11-4
1970	**Magic Flute**	N Murless	A Barclay	13-8
1971	**Waterloo**	J Watts	E Hide	100-30
1972	**Jacinth**	B Hobbs	J Gorton	9-2
1973	**Gentle Thoughts**	T Curtin	W Pyers	9-1
1974	**Cry Of Truth**	B Hobbs	J Gorton	4-1

1975	**Pasty**	P Walwyn	P Eddery	9-1
1976	**Durtal**	B Hills	L Piggott	5-1
1977	**Sookera**	DK Weld	W Swinburn	3-1
1978	**Devon Ditty**	T Jones	G Starkey	11-8
1979	**Mrs Penny**	I Balding	J Matthias	7-1
1980	**Marwell**	M Stoute	L Piggott	4-9
1981	**Woodstream**	MV O'Brien	P Eddery	5-2
1982	**Ma Biche**	Mme C Head	F Head	11-4
1983	**Desirable**	B Hills	S Cauthen	12-1

Run as Cheveley Park Stakes from 1870-1972.

WILLIAM HILL MIDDLE PARK STAKES

Newmarket 6f 2-y-o c

		Trainer	Jockey	SP
1946	**Saravan**	F Butters	C Elliott	100-8
1947	**The Cobbler**	F Darling	G Richards	8-11
1948	**Abernant**	N Murless	G Richards	1-7
1949	**Masked Light**	N Scobie	D Smith	7-2
1950	**Big Dipper**	C B-Rochfort	W Carr	2-5
1951	**King's Bench**	M Feakes	C Elliott	7-2
1952	**Nearula**	C Elsey	E Britt	13-2
1953	**Royal Challenger**	P Beasley	G Richards	4-1
1954	**Our Babu**	G Brooke	D Smith	6-1
1955	**Buisson Ardent**	A Head	D Smith	9-2
1956	**Pipe Of Peace**	Sir G Richards	A Breasley	8-1
1957	**Major Portion**	T Leader	E Smith	11-2
1958	**Masham**	G Brooke	D Smith	2-1
1959	**Venture VII**	A Head	G Moore	1-4
1960	**Skymaster**	W Smyth	A Breasley	100-30
1961	**Gustav**	J Tree	J Lindley	100-6
1962	**Crocket**	G Brooke	E Smith	5-4
1963	**Showdown**	F Winter	D Smith	100-30
1964	**Spanish Express**	L Hall	J Mercer	9-1
1965	**Track Spare**	R Mason	J Lindley	10-1
1966	**Bold Lad**	PJ Prendergast	D Lake	2-7
1967	**Petingo**	F Armstrong	L Piggott	1-4
1968	**Right Tack**	J Sutcliffe Jr	G Lewis	11-2
1969	**Huntercombe**	A Budgett	E Johnson	3-1
1970	**Brigadier Gerard**	W Hern	J Mercer	9-2
1971	**Sharpen Up**	B van Cutsem	W Carson	5-6
1972	**Tudenham**	Denys Smith	J Lindley	4-1
1973	**Habat**	P Walwyn	P Eddery	4-6
1974	**Steel Heart**	D Weld	L Piggott	10-11
1975	**Hittite Glory**	A Breasley	F Durr	9-2
1976	**Tachypous**	B Hobbs	G Lewis	5-1
1977	**Formidable**	P Walwyn	P Eddery	15-8
1978	**Junius**	MV O'Brien	L Piggott	7-1

1979	**Known Fact**	J Tree	W Carson	10-1
1980	**Mattaboy**	R Armstrong	L Piggott	7-1
1981	**Cajun**	H Cecil	L Piggott	20-1
1982	**Diesis**	H Cecil	L Piggott	10-11
1983	**Creag-An-Sgor**	C Nelson	S Cauthen	50-1

First run in 1866. Run as Middle Park Plate from 1866 to 1921, as Middle Park Stakes from 1922-72.

WILLIAM HILL CAMBRIDGESHIRE HANDICAP

Newmarket 1m 1f

		Trainer	Jockey	SP
1946	**Sayani**	J Lieux	W Johnstone	25-1
1947	**Fairey Fulmar**	O Bell	T Gosling	28-1
1948	**Sterope**	P Beasley	D Schofield	25-1
1949	**Sterope**	P Beasley	C Elliott	25-1
1950	**Kelling**	A Waugh	D Smith	100-1
1951	**Fleeting Moment**	T Bartlam	A Breasley	28-1
1952	**Richer**	S Ingham	K Gethin	100-6
1953	**Jupiter**	P Beasley	G Richards	100-6
1954	**Minstrel**	J Jarvis	C Gaston	66-1
1955	**Retrial**	C B-Rochfort	P Robinson	18-1
1956	**Loppylugs**	J Beary	E Smith	100-7
1957	**Stephanotis**	J Rogers	W Carr	100-6
1958	**London Cry**	Sir G Richards	A Breasley	22-1
1959	**Rexequus**	G Boyd	N Stirk	25-1
1960	**Midsummer Night II**	P H-Bass	D Keith	40-1
1961	**Violetta**	H Wragg	C Parkes	33-1
1961	**Henry The Seventh**	W Elsey	E Hide	100-8
1962	**Hidden Meaning**	H Leader	A Breasley	7-1
1963	**Commander-In-Chief**	E Cousins	F Durr	100-7
1964	**Hasty Cloud**	H Wallington	J Wilson	100-8
1965	**Tarquogan**	S McGrath	W Williamson	100-8
1966	**Dites**	H Leader	D Maitland	33-1
1967	**Lacquer**	H Wragg	R Hutchinson	20-1
1968	**Emerilo**	P Allden	M Thomas	20-1
1969	**Prince de Galles**	P Robinson	F Durr	5-2
1970	**Prince de Galles**	P Robinson	F Durr	6-1
1971	**King Midas**	D Candy	D Cullen	10-1
1972	**Negus**	D Candy	P Waldron	16-1
1973	**Siliciana**	I Balding	G Lewis	14-1
1974	**Flying Nelly**	W Wightman	D Maitland	22-1
1975	**Lottogift**	D Hanley	R Wernham	33-1
1976	**Intermission**	M Stoute	G Starkey	14-1
1977	**Sin Timon**	J Hindley	A Kimberley	18-1

1978	**Baronet**	C Benstead	B Rouse	12-1
1979	**Smartset**	R Johnson Houghton	J Reid	33-1
1980	**Baronet**	C Benstead	B Rouse	22-1
1981	**Braughing**	C Brittain	S Cauthen	50-1
1982	**Century City**	L Cumani	J Mercer	20-1
1983	**Sagamore**	F Durr	ML Thomas	35-1

First run in 1839 as Cambridgeshire Stakes. From 1971-77 run as the Irish Sweeps Cambridgeshire Handicap. Renamed 1978.

WILLIAM HILL DEWHURST STAKES

Newmarket 7f 2-y-o

		Trainer	Jockey	SP
1946	**Migoli**	F Butters	G Richards	5-1
1947	**Pride Of India**	J Watts	J Sime	5-2
1948	**Royal Forest**	N Murless	G Richards	5-4
1949	**Emperor II**	C Semblat	C Elliott	7-2
1950	**Turco II**	C B-Rochfort	W Carr	11-8
1951	**Marsyad**	C Semblat	W Johnstone	7-1
1952	**Pinza**	N Bertie	G Richards	Evens
1953	**Infatuation**	V Smyth	K Gethin	11-8
1954	**My Smokey**	J Watts	D Smith	7-2
1955	**Darcian**	H Cottrill	W Snaith	7-1
1956	**Crepello**	N Murless	L Piggott	1-2
1957	**Torbella III**	W Clout	A Breasley	9-4
1958	**Billum**	C Elsey	E Hide	6-1
1959	**Ancient Lights**	T Leader	E Smith	100-7
1960	**Bounteous**	P Beasley	J Sime	2-1
1961	**River Chanter**	G Todd	J Mercer	100-30
1962	**Follow Suit**	N Murless	L Piggott	10-1
1963	**King's Lane**	S Hall	J Sime	10-1
1964	**Silly Season**	I Balding	G Lewis	13-2
1965	**Pretendre**	J Jarvis	R Hutchinson	11-2
1966	**Dart Board**	Sir G Richards	D Smith	10-1
1967	**Hametus**	W Nightingall	F Durr	100-9
1968	**Ribofilio**	R Johnson Houghton	L Piggott	8-11
1969	**Nijinsky**	MV O'Brien	L Piggott	1-3
1970	**Mill Reef**	I Balding	G Lewis	4-7
1971	**Crowned Prince**	B van Cutsem	L Piggott	4-9
1972	**Lunchtime**	P Walwyn	P Eddery	11-8
1973	**Cellini**	MV O'Brien	L Piggott	40-85
1974	**Grundy**	P Walwyn	P Eddery	6-5
1975	**Wollow**	H Cecil	G Dettori	6-4
1976	**The Minstrel**	MV O'Brien	L Piggott	4-6
1977	**Try My Best**	MV O'Brien	P Eddery	4-5

1978	**Tromos**	B Hobbs	J Lynch	11-4
1979	**Monteverdi**	MV O'Brien	L Piggott	15-8
1980	**Storm Bird**	MV O'Brien	P Eddery	4-5
1981	**Wind And Wuthering**	H Candy	P Waldron	11-1
1982	**Diesis**	H Cecil	L Piggott	2-1
1983	**El Gran Senor**	MV O'Brien	P Eddery	7-4

Run as Dewhurst Stakes from 1875 to 1972.

DUBAI CHAMPION STAKES

Newmarket 1¼ m

		Trainer	Jockey	SP
1946	**Honeyway**	J Jarvis	E Smith	8-1
1947	**Migoli**	F Butters	G Richards	Evens
1948	**Solar Slipper**	H Smyth	E Smith	6-1
1949	**Djeddah**	C Semblat	C Elliott	4-6
1950	**Peter Flower**	J Jarvis	W Rickaby	3-1
1951	**Dynamiter**	C Semblat	C Elliott	100-8
1952	**Dynamiter**	J Glynn	C Elliott	4-5
1953	**Nearula**	C Elsey	E Britt	4-1
1954	**Narrator**	H Cottrill	F Barlow	20-1
1955	**Hafiz II**	A Head	R Poincelet	100-30
1956	**Hugh Lupus**	N Murless	W Johnstone	3-1
1957	**Rose Royale II**	A Head	J Massard	5-2
1958	**Bella Paola**	F Mathet	G Lequeux	4-1
1959	**Petite Etoile**	N Murless	L Piggott	2-11
1960	**Marguerite Vernaut**	U Penco	E Camici	9-4
1961	**Bobar II**	R Corme	M Garcia	100-8
1962	**Arctic Storm**	J Oxx	W Williamson	6-1
1963	**Hula Dancer**	E Pollet	J Deforge	9-2
1964	**Baldric II**	E Fellows	W Pyers	7-2
1965	**Silly Season**	I Balding	G Lewis	100-8
1966	**Pieces Of Eight**	MV O'Brien	L Piggott	5-4
1967	**Reform**	Sir G Richards	A Breasley	100-30
1968	**Sir Ivor**	MV O'Brien	L Piggott	8-11
1969	**Flossy**	F Boutin	J Deforge	100-7
1970	**Lorenzaccio**	N Murless	G Lewis	100-7
1971	**Brigadier Gerard**	W Hern	J Mercer	1-2
1972	**Brigadier Gerard**	W Hern	J Mercer	1-3
1973	**Hurry Harriet**	P Mullins	J Cruguet	33-1
1974	**Giacometti**	Ryan Price	L Piggott	4-1
1975	**Rose Bowl**	R Johnson Houghton	W Carson	11-2
1976	**Vitiges**	P Walwyn	P Eddery	22-1
1977	**Flying Water**	A Penna	Y Saint-Martin	9-1

1978	**Swiss Maid**	P Kelleway	G Starkey	9-1
1979	**Northern Baby**	F Boutin	P Paquet	9-1
1980	**Cairn Rouge**	M Cunningham	A Murray	6-1
1981	**Vayrann**	F Mathet	Y Saint-Martin	15-2
1982	**Time Charter**	H Candy	W Newnes	9-2
1983	**Cormorant Wood**	B Hills	S Cauthen	18-1

First run in 1877 as Champion Stakes. Renamed in 1982.

TOTE CESAREWITCH HANDICAP

Newmarket 2¼ m

		Trainer	Jockey	SP
1946	**Monsieur L'Amiral**	E Charlier	H Wragg	33-1
1947	**Whiteway**	W Pratt	W Evans	100-8
1948	**Woodburn**	C Elsey	E Britt	100-9
1949	**Strathspey**	N Cannon	E Smith	25-1
1950	**Above Board**	C B-Rochfort	E Smith	18-1
1951	**Three Cheers**	P Thrale	E Mercer	17-2
1952	**Flush Royal**	J Fawcus	W Nevett	33-1
1953	**Chantrey**	S Ingham	K Gethin	4-1
1954	**French Design**	G Todd	D Smith	100-6
1955	**Curry**	F Armstrong	P Tulk	100-6
1956	**Prelone**	W Hide	E Hide	20-1
1957	**Sandiacre**	W Dutton	D Smith	100-8
1958	**Morecambe**	S Hall	J Sime	15-2
1959	**Come To Daddy**	W Lyde	D Smith	6-1
1960	**Alcove**	J Watts	D Smith	100-30
1961	**Avon's Pride**	W Hern	E Smith	100-8
1962	**Golden Fire**	D Marks	D Yates	25-1
1963	**Utrillo**	Ryan Price	J Sime	100-8
1964	**Grey Of Falloden**	W Hern	J Mercer	20-1
1965	**Mintmaster**	A Cooper	J Sime	13-2
1966	**Persian Lancer**	Ryan Price	D Smith	100-7
1967	**Boismoss**	MW Easterby	E Johnson	13-1
1968	**Major Rose**	Ryan Price	L Piggott	9-1
1969	**Floridian**	L Shedden	D McKay	20-1
1970	**Scoria**	C Crossley	D McKay	33-1
1971	**Orosio**	H Cecil	G Lewis	5-1
1972	**Cider With Rosie**	S Ingham	M Thomas	14-1
1973	**Flash Imp**	R Smyth	T Cain	25-1
1974	**Ocean King**	A Pitt	T Carter	25-1
1975	**Shantallah**	H Wragg	B Taylor	7-1
1976	**John Cherry**	J Tree	L Piggott	13-2
1977	**Assured**	H Candy	P Waldron	10-1
1978	**Centurion**	I Balding	J Matthias	9-2
1979	**Sir Michael**	G Huffer	M Rimmer	10-1
1980	**Popsi's Joy**	M Haynes	L Piggott	10-1
1981	**Halsbury**	P Walwyn	J Mercer	14-1

| 1982 | **Mountain Lodge** | J Dunlop | W Carson | 9-1 |
| 1983 | **Bajan Sunshine** | R Simpson | B Rouse | 7-1 |

First run in 1839 as Cesarewitch Stakes. Renamed in 1978.

WILLIAM HILL FUTURITY

Doncaster 1m 2-y-o

		Trainer	Jockey	SP
1961	**Miralgo**	H Wragg	W Williamson	10-1
1962	**Noblesse**	PJ Prendergast	G Bougoure	11-10
1963	**Pushful**	S Meaney	W Carr	100-6
1964	**Hardicanute**	PJ Prendergast	W Williamson	13-8
1965	**Pretendre**	J Jarvis	R Hutchinson	6-1
1966	**Ribocco**	R Johnson Houghton	L Piggott	4-9
1967	**Vaguely Noble**	W Wharton	W Williamson	8-1
1968	**The Elk**	J Tree	W Pyers	10-1
1969	**Approval**	H Cecil	D Keith	5-1
1970	**Linden Tree**	P Walwyn	D Keith	25-1
1971	**High Top**	B van Cutsem	W Carson	11-2
1972	**Noble Decree**	B van Cutsem	L Piggott	8-1
1973	**Apalachee**	MV O'Brien	L Piggott	Evens
1974	**Green Dancer**	A Head	F Head	7-2
1975	**Take Your Place**	H Cecil	G Dettori	4-1
1976	**Sporting Yankee**	P Walwyn	P Eddery	9-2
1977	**Dactylographer**	P Walwyn	P Eddery	100-30
1978	**Sandy Creek**	C Collins	C Roche	15-1
1979	**Hello Gorgeous**	H Cecil	J Mercer	11-8
1980	**Beldale Flutter**	M Jarvis	P Eddery	14-1
1981	**Count Pahlen**	B Hobbs	G Baxter	25-1
1982	**Dunbeath**	H Cecil	L Piggott	4-7
1983	**Alphabatim**	G Harwood	G Starkey	9-2

Originally run as Timeform Gold Cup from 1961-64 and then Observer Gold Cup from 1965-75. Renamed in 1976.

Henry Cecil, trainer of four successes in the William Hill Futurity.

OVERSEAS RACES

Ireland

GOFFS IRISH 1,000 GUINEAS

The Curragh 1m

		Trainer	Jockey	SP
1960	Zenobia	T Shaw	L Ward	100-8
1961	Lady Senator	P Ashworth	T Gosling	6-4
1962	Shandon Belle	R Fetherstonhaugh	TP Burns	20-1
1963	Gazpacho	PJ Prendergast	F Palmer	9-1
1964	Royal Danseuse	S McGrath	J Roe	7-4
1965	Ardent Dancer	T Gosling	W Rickaby	5-1
1966	Valoris	MV O'Brien	J Power	9-1
1967	Lacquer	H Wragg	R Hutchinson	4-1
1968	Front Row	R Jarvis	E Eldin	7-1
1969	Wenduyne	PJ Prendergast	W Williamson	2-1
1970	Black Satin	J Dunlop	R Hutchinson	3-1
1971	Favoletta	H Wragg	L Piggott	5-2
1972	Pidget	K Prendergast	W Swinburn	20-1
1973	Cloonagh	H Cecil	G Starkey	7-1
1974	Gaily	W Hern	R Hutchinson	11-5
1975	Miralia	Sir H Nugent	RF Parnell	14-1
1976	Sarah Siddons	PJ Prendergast	G Roche	2-1
1977	Lady Capulet	MV O'Brien	T Murphy	16-1
1978	More So	PJ Prendergast	C Roche	2-1
1979	Godetia	MV O'Brien	L Piggott	4-6
1980	Gairn Rouge	M Cunningham	A Murray	5-1
1981	Arctique Royale	K Prendergast	G Curran	7-1
1982	Prince's Polly	D Weld	W Swinburn	12-1
1983	L'Attrayante	O Douieb	A Badel	4-1

Run until 1979 as Irish 1,000 Guineas. Renamed in 1980.

AIRLIE-COOLMORE IRISH 2,000 GUINEAS

The Curragh 1m

		Trainer	Jockey	SP
1960	Kythnos	PJ Prendergast	R Hutchinson	5-4
1961	Light Year	A O'Brien	G Bougoure	6-1
1962	Arctic Storm	J Oxx	W Williamson	20-1
1963	Linacre	PJ Prendergast	P Matthews	40-1
1964	Santa Claus	J Rogers	W Burke	Evens
1965	Green Banner	K Kerr	N Brennan	100-7

1966	**Paveh**	T Ainsworth	TP Burns	9-1
1967	**Atherstone**	S Quirke	R Parnell	100-7
1968	**Mistigo**	S Quirke	R Parnell	10-1
1969	**Right Tack**	J Sutcliffe	G Lewis	Evens
1970	**Decies**	B van Cutsem	L Piggott	8-13
1971	**King's Company**	G Robinson	F Head	9-2
1972	**Ballymore**	PJ Prendergast	C Roche	33-1
1973	**Sharp Edge**	W Hern	J Mercer	5-2
1974	**Furry Glen**	S McGrath	G McGrath	10-1
1975	**Grundy**	P Walwyn	P Eddery	10-11
1976	**Northern Treasure**	K Prendergast	G Curran	33-1
1977	**Pampapaul**	HV Murless	G Dettori	16-1
1978	**Jaazeiro**	MV O'Brien	L Piggott	11-4
1979	**Dickens Hill**	M O'Toole	A Murray	5-2
1980	**Nikoli**	PJ Prendergast	C Roche	5-1
1981	**King's Lake**	MV O'Brien	P Eddery	5-1
1982	**Dara Monarch**	L Browne	MJ Kinane	20-1
1983	**Wassl**	J Dunlop	A Murray	12-1

Renamed in 1980.

IRISH SWEEPS DERBY

The Curragh 1½m 3-y-o

		Trainer	Jockey	SP
1960	**Chamour**	A O'Brien	G Bougoure	3-1
1961	**Your Highness**	H Cottrill	H Holmes	33-1
1962	**Tambourine II**	E Pollet	R Poincelet	15-2
1963	**Ragusa**	PJ Prendergast	G Bougoure	100-7
1964	**Santa Claus**	J Rogers	W Burke	4-7
1965	**Meadow Court**	PJ Prendergast	L Piggott	11-10
1966	**Sodium**	G Todd	F Durr	13-2
1967	**Ribocco**	R Johnson Houghton	L Piggott	5-2
1968	**Ribero**	R Johnson Houghton	L Piggott	100-6
1969	**Prince Regent**	E Pollet	G Lewis	7-2
1970	**Nijinsky**	MV O'Brien	L Ward	4-11
1971	**Irish Ball**	P Lallie	A Gibert	7-2
1972	**Steel Pulse**	A Breasley	W Williamson	10-1
1973	**Weaver's Hall**	S McGrath	G McGrath	33-1
1974	**English Prince**	P Walwyn	Y Saint-Martin	8-1
1975	**Grundy**	P Walwyn	P Eddery	9-10
1976	**Malacate**	F Boutin	P Paquet	5-1
1977	**The Minstrel**	MV O'Brien	L Piggott	11-10
1978	**Shirley Heights**	J Dunlop	G Starkey	5-4
1979	**Troy**	W Hern	W Carson	4-9
1980	**Tyrnavos**	B Hobbs	A Murray	25-1

1981	**Shergar**	M Stoute	L Piggott	1-3
1982	**Assert**	D O'Brien	C Roche	4-7
1983	**Shareef Dancer**	M Stoute	WR Swinburn	8-1

First run in 1866.

IRISH GUINNESS OAKS

The Curragh 1½m 3-y-o f

		Trainer	Jockey	SP
1960	**Lynchris**	J Oxx	W Williamson	11-4
1961	**Ambergris**	H Wragg	J Lindley	6-4
1962	**French Cream**	G Brooke	W Rickaby	100-9
1963	**Hibernia III**	J Oxx	W Williamson	6-4
1964	**Ancasta**	MV O'Brien	J Purtell	3-1
1965	**Aurabella**	MV O'Brien	L Ward	22-1
1966	**Merry Mate**	J Oxx	W Williamson	100-9
1967	**Pampalina**	J Oxx	J Roe	100-8
1968	**Celina**	N Murless	A Barclay	4-1
1969	**Gaia**	MV O'Brien	L Ward	9-1
1970	Santa Tina	C Millbank	L Piggott	5-2
1971	**Altesse Royale**	N Murless	G Lewis	1-2
1972	**Regal Exception**	J Fellows	M Philipperon	4-1
1973	**Dahlia**	M Zilber	W Pyers	8-1
1974	**Dibidale**	B Hills	W Carson	7-4
1975	**Juliette Marny**	J Tree	L Piggott	5-2
1976	**Lagunette**	F Boutin	P Paquet	3-1
1977	**Olwyn**	R Boss	J Lynch	11-1
1978	**Fair Salinia**	M Stoute	G Starkey	3-1
1979	**Godetia**	MV O'Brien	L Piggott	6-4
1980	**Shoot A Line**	W Hern	W Carson	6-4
1981	**Blue Wind**	D Weld	W Swinburn	4-6
1982	**Swiftfoot**	W Hern	W Carson	4-1
1983	**Give Thanks**	J Bolger	D Gillespie	7-4

First run in 1895. Run as Irish Oaks until 1962.

JEFFERSON SMURFIT MEMORIAL IRISH ST LEGER

The Curragh 1¾m

		Trainer	Jockey	SP
1960	**Lynchris**	J Oxx	W Williamson	4-6
1961	**Vimadee**	T Burns	TP Burns	100-9
1962	**Arctic Vale**	PJ Prendergast	P Matthews	40-1

1963	**Christmas Island**	PJ Prendergast	G Bougoure	6-1
1964	**Biscayne**	J Oxx	W Williamson	4-1
1965	**Craighouse**	W Hern	J Mercer	6-1
1966	**White Gloves**	MV O'Brien	L Ward	4-1
1967	**Dan Kano**	J Lenehan	L Piggott	Evens
1968	**Giolla Mear**	M Hurley	P Berry	8-1
1969	**Reindeer**	MV O'Brien	L Ward	5-2
1970	**Allangrange**	S McGrath	G McGrath	9-1
1971	**Parnell**	S Quirke	A Simpson	11-5
1972	**Pidget**	K Prendergast	T Burns	13-2
1973	**Conor Pass**	K Prendergast	P Jarman	5-1
1974	**Mistigri**	PJ Prendergast	C Roche	9-1
1975	**Caucasus**	MV O'Brien	L Piggott	3-1
1976	**Meneval**	MV O'Brien	L Piggott	5-4
1977	**Transworld**	MV O'Brien	T Murphy	13-2
1978	**M-Lolshan**	Ryan Price	B Taylor	2-1
1979	**Niniski**	W Hern	W Carson	11-10
1980	**Gonzales**	MV O'Brien	R Carroll	4-7
1981	**Protection Racket**	J Hindley	B Taylor	6-4
1982	**Touching Wood**	H Thomson Jones	P Cook	5-4
1983	**Mountain Lodge**	J Dunlop	D Gillespie	13-2

First run in 1915. Run as Irish St Leger until 1981.

France

PRIX DU JOCKEY-CLUB

Chantilly 1½m

		Trainer	Jockey
1960	**Charlottesville**	A Head	G Moore
1961	**Right Royal V**	E Pollet	R Poincelet
1962	**Val de Loir**	M Bonaventure	F Palmer
1963	**Sanctus**	E Pollet	M Larraun
1964	**Le Fabuleux**	W Head	J Massard
1965	**Reliance II**	F Mathet	Y Saint-Martin
1966	**Nelcius**	M Clement	Y Saint-Martin
1967	**Astec**	A Mieux	A Jezequal
1968	**Tapalque**	F Mathet	Y Saint-Martin
1969	**Goodly**	W Head	F Head
1970	**Sassafras**	F Mathet	Y Saint-Martin
1971	**Rheffic**	F Mathet	W Pyers
1972	**Hard To Beat**	R Carver	L Piggott
1973	**Roi Lear**	A Head	F Head
1974	**Caracolero**	F Boutin	P Paquet
1975	**Val de l'Orne**	A Head	F Head
1976	**Youth**	M Zilber	F Head
1977	**Crystal Palace**	F Mathet	G Dubroeucq
1978	**Acamas**	G Bonaventure	Y Saint-Martin
1979	**Top Ville**	F Mathet	Y Saint-Martin

1980	**Policeman**	C Millbank	W Carson
1981	**Bikala**	P Biancone	S Gorli
1982	**Assert**	D O'Brien	C Roche
1983	**Caerleon**	MV O'Brien	P Eddery

PRIX DE DIANE HERMES

Chantilly 1m 2f 110y f

		Trainer	Jockey
1960	**Timandra**	G Watson	G Boullenger
1961	**Hermieres**	G Watson	G Boullenger
1962	**Le Sega**	F Mathet	Y Saint-Martin
1963	**Belle Ferroniere**	R Carver	J Carver
1964	**Belle Sicambre**	C Bartholomew	M Garcia
1965	**Blabal**	H Velavaud	M Depalmas
1966	**Fine Pearl**	F Palmer	J Massard
1967	**Gazala**	J Cunnington Jr	M Philipperon
1968	**Roseliere**	G Bridgland	Y Josse
1969	**Crepellana**	M Boussac	R Poincelet
1970	**Sweet Mimosa**	S McGrath	W Williamson
1971	**Pistol Packer**	A Head	F Head
1972	**Rescousse**	G Watson	Y Saint-Martin
1973	**Allez France**	A Klimscha	Y Saint-Martin
1974	**Highclere**	W Hern	J Mercer
1975	No Race		
1976	**Pawneese**	A Penna	Y Saint-Martin
1977	**Madelia**	A Penna	Y Saint-Martin
1978	**Reine de Saba**	A Head	F Head
1979	**Dunette**	E Chevalier du Fau	G Doleuze
1980	**Mrs Penny**	I Balding	L Piggott
1981	**Madam Gay**	P Kelleway	L Piggott
1982	**Harbour**	Mme C Head	F Head
1983	**Escaline**	J Fellows	GW Moore

Originally called Prix de Diane.
Called Prix de Diane de Revlon from 1977–81. Renamed in 1982.

TRUSTHOUSE FORTE PRIX DE L'ARC DE TRIOMPHE

Longchamp 1½m

		Trainer	Jockey
1960	**Puissant Chef**	C Bartholomew	M Garcia
1961	**Molvedo**	A Maggi	E Camici
1962	**Soltikoff**	R Pelat	M Depalmas
1963	**Exbury**	G Watson	J Deforge

1964	**Prince Royal II**	G Bridgland	R Poincelet
1965	**Sea Bird II**	E Pollet	T Glennon
1966	**Bon Mot III**	W Head	F Head
1967	**Topyo**	C Bartholomew	W Pyers
1968	**Vaguely Noble**	E Pollet	W Williamson
1969	**Levmoss**	S McGrath	W Williamson
1970	**Sassafras**	F Mathet	Y Saint-Martin
1971	**Mill Reef**	I Balding	G Lewis
1972	**San San**	A Penna	F Head
1973	**Rheingold**	B Hills	L Piggott
1974	**Allez France**	A Penna	Y Saint-Martin
1975	**Star Appeal**	T Grieper	G Starkey
1976	**Ivanjica**	A Head	F Head
1977	**Alleged**	MV O'Brien	L Piggott
1978	**Alleged**	MV O'Brien	L Piggott
1979	**Three Troikas**	Mme C Head	F Head
1980	**Detroit**	O Douieb	P Eddery
1981	**Gold River**	A Head	GW Moore
1982	**Akiyda**	F Mathet	Y Saint-Martin
1983	**All Along**	P-L Biancone	W Swinburn

First run in 1920 as Prix de L'Arc de Triomphe. Renamed in 1982.

USA

WASHINGTON INTERNATIONAL

Laurel 1½m

		Trainer	**Jockey**
1960	**Bald Eagle**	W Stephens	M Ycaza
1961	**TV Lark**	P Parker	J Longden
1962	**Match III**	F Mathet	Y Saint-Martin
1963	**Mongo**	F Bonsal	W Chambers
1964	**Kelso**	C Hanford	I Valenzuela
1965	**Diatome**	G Watson	J Deforge
1966	**Behistoun**	J Lieux	J Deforge
1967	**Fort Marcy**	E Burch	M Ycaza
1968	**Sir Ivor**	MV O'Brien	L Piggott
1969	**Karabas**	B van Cutsem	L Piggott
1970	**Fort Marcy**	E Burch	J Velasquez
1971	**Run The Gantlet**	E Burch	P Woodhouse
1972	**Droll Role**	T Kelly	B Baeza
1973	**Dahlia**	M Zilber	W Pyers
1974	**Admetus**	J Cunnington Jr	M Philipperon
1975	**Nobiliary**	M Zilber	S Hawley
1976	**Youth**	M Zilber	S Hawley
1977	**Johny D**	M Kay	S Cauthen
1978	**Mac Diarmida**	F Schulhofer	J Cruguet
1979	**Bowl Game**	J Graver	J Velasquez
1980	**Argument**	M Zilber	L Piggott

1981	**Providential II**	C Whittingham	A Lequeux
1982	**April Run**	F Boutin	C Asmussen
1983	**All Along**	P-L Biancone	W Swinburn

AUSTRALIA

THE MELBOURNE CUP

1861	Archer	1905	Blue Spec
1862	Archer	1906	Poseidon
1863	Banker	1907	Apologue
1864	Lantern	1908	Lord Nolan
1865	Toryboy	1909	Prince Foote
1866	The Barb	1910	Comedy King
1867	Tim Whiffler	1911	The Parisian
1868	Glencoe	1912	Piastre
1869	Warrior	1913	Positanus
1870	Nimblefoot	1914	Kingsburgh
1871	The Pearl	1915	Patrobas
1872	Thee Quack	1916	Sasanof
1873	Don Juan	1917	Westcourt
1874	Haricot	1918	Night Watch
1875	Wollomai	1919	Artilleryman
1876	Briseis	1920	Poitrel
1877	Chester	1921	Sister Olive
1878	Calamia	1922	King Ingoda
1879	Darriwell	1923	Bitalli
1880	Grand Flaneur	1924	Backwood
1881	Zulu	1925	Windbag
1882	The Assyrian	1926	Spearfelt
1883	Martini-Henry	1927	Trivalve
1884	Malua	1928	Statesman
1885	Sheet Anchor	1929	Nightmarch
1886	Arsenal	1930	Phar Lap
1887	Dunlop	1931	White Nose
1888	Mentor	1932	Peter Pan
1889	Bravo	1933	Hall Mark
1890	Carbine	1934	Peter Pan
1891	Malvolio	1935	Marabou
1892	Glenloth	1936	Wotan
1893	Tarcoola	1937	The Trumps
1894	Patron	1938	Catalogue
1895	Auraria	1939	Rivette
1896	Newhaven	1940	Old Rowley
1897	Gaulus	1941	Skipton
1898	The Grafter	1942	Colonus
1899	Merriwee	1943	Dark Felt
1900	Clean Sweep	1944	Sirius
1901	Revenue	1945	Rainbird
1902	The Victory	1946	Russia
1903	Lord Cardigan	1947	Hiraji
1904	Acrasia	1948	Rimfire

1949	Foxzami	1967	Red Handed
1950	Comic Court	1968	Rain Lover
1951	Delta	1969	Rain Lover
1952	Dalray	1970	Baghdad Note
1953	Wodalla	1971	Silver Knight
1954	Rising Fast	1972	Pipine Lane
1955	Toparoa	1973	Gala Supreme
1956	Evening Pearl	1974	Think Big
1957	Straight Draw	1975	Think Big
1958	Baystone	1976	Van Der Hum
1959	Macdougal	1977	Gold and Black
1960	Hi Jinx	1978	Arwon
1961	Lord Fury	1979	Hyperno
1962	Even Stevens	1980	Beldale Ball
1963	Gatum Gatum	1981	Just A Dash
1964	Polo Prince	1982	Gurner's Lane
1965	Light Fingers	1983	Kiwi
1966	Galilee		

Gordon Richards after winning the 1953 Derby on Pinza.

THE GREATS

Howard Wright

OWNERS

LORD DERBY (1865-1948)

The 17th Earl of Derby inherited and built on his father's love of racing and breeding. As an owner his colours of black jacket and white cap were successful in 20 Classics, including three—Sansovino (1924), Hyperion (1933) and Watling Street (1942)—in the world's most famous Flat race, the Derby, named after the 12th Earl. His most prolific Classic successes were in the 1,000 Guineas, which he won seven times between 1916 and 1945.

He was one of the greatest owner-breeders of the 20th century, operating from the Stanley House Stud at Newmarket, and among the best stallions he owned were Chaucer, Swynford, Phalaris, Pharos, Fairway and Hyperion. His last notable winner was Alycidon, who captured the Ascot, Goodwood and Doncaster Cups in 1948, the year of his death, when his racing interests were taken over by his grandson, the 18th Earl.

JOEL FAMILY

JB Joel (1862-1940) registered his colours of black jacket and scarlet cap in 1900, from when the South African diamond millionaire was represented by 11 Classic winners, including the Derby with Sunstar (1911) and Humorist (1921). His brother 'Solly' Joel (1865-1931) owned one Classic winner, Pommern, who took the Triple Crown of 2,000 Guineas, Derby and St Leger in 1915. Solly's son, Stanhope Joel (1903-1976), lived in the Bahamas and was rarely seen in Britain, but he maintained a considerable racing interest and had his most important successes with Chamossaire (St Leger) and Busted (Eclipse Stakes and King George VI and Queen Elizabeth Stakes).

The Aga Khan leading in Mahmoud after winning The Derby.

Jim Joel (born 1894) inherited the Childwick Bury Stud from his father JB Joel, whose colours he also took over, and he revived the family's racing fortunes, though his first two Classic winners were separated by 23 years—Picture Play (1,000 Guineas) and Royal Palace (2,000 Guineas and Derby). These were followed by Light Cavalry (St Leger) and Fairy Footsteps (1,000 Guineas), while West Side Story and Connaught were second in Classics.

LORD WOOLAVINGTON (1849-1935)

Captain Cuttle (1922) and Coronach (1926) brought Lord Woolavington his two Derby successes, but Hurry On (sire of both these horses), whom he bought for 500 guineas, was easily the best racer to carry his colours. He founded the whisky firm of James Buchanan and Co.

AGA KHAN (1877-1957)

The Aga Khan was the outstanding figure in European racing for 25 years from 1922, the first year he raced in England. His horses were trained by Richard Dawson, Frank Butters, Marcus Marsh and Noel Murless until in 1954 he transferred his interests to France because of lower costs and a higher level of prize money.

He shares with Lord Egremont the distinction of having won the Derby five times—Blenheim (1930), Bahram (1935), Mahmoud (1936), My Love (1948) and Tulyar (1952). He had 11 other Classic successes, and when Firdaussi won the St Leger in 1932 the Aga Khan owned four of the first five finishers.

The fillies Mumtaz Mahal, Cos and Teresina became foundation mares for the chain of studs he established in Ireland and France, but acutely aware of the commercial aspect of racing, he was criticised for selling abroad as stallions some of his best racers. He sold all his Derby winners, and the export of Blenheim, Bahram and Mahmoud proved a hard blow to the British bloodstock industry, surpassed only by the sale of Nasrullah to the United States.

When the Aga Khan died, his son Prince Aly Khan (1911-1960) took over his racing interests and in 1959 became the first owner to win more than £100,000 in stakes in Britain with the classic winners Taboun (2,000 Guineas) and Petite Etoile (1,000 Guineas and Oaks) among them. Following Prince Aly's death in a car accident, the family's racing involvement waned, but it was revived in the 1970s when the Aga Khan (born 1936) built a new stud in Normandy and later bought the bloodstock of the late Mme Dupre and M Marcel Boussac. In 1979 he won the French Derby with Top Ville. In 1981 the Derby with Shergar and the following year the Arc de Triomphe with Akiyda.

JOHN ARTHUR DEWAR (1891-1954)

John Dewar had little interest in racing until at the age of 40 he inherited from an uncle a string of horses and a stud. Among the inheritance was Cameronian, who went on to win the 2,000 Guineas and Derby. This developed Dewar's involvement, and his other Classic winners were Tudor Minstrel (2,000 Guineas), Commotion (Oaks) and Festoon (1,000 Guineas). When his thoroughbred interests were sold on his death, they created enormous interest and made a total of more than £418,000.

LORD ROSEBERY (1882-1974)

The 6th Earl of Rosebery failed to match the score of 11 Classic winners that made his father one of the prominent owner-breeders at the turn of the 20th century, but the five such winners he did own included Blue Peter, one of the best horses of the time. Blue Peter (1939) and Ocean Swell (1944) were Lord Rosebery's Derby winners, and he achieved one of his prime ambitions when Sleeping Partner won the Oaks in 1969, after having had six placings in the race. His horses were trained by Sir Jack Jarvis until the latter's death in 1968. Lord Rosebery inherited the Mentmore Stud from his father in 1929, but on his own death the property was sold and his colours of primrose, rose hoops and cap disappeared from the Turf.

MISS DOROTHY PAGET (1905-60)

Though she was perhaps better known for runners over jumps, the eccentric Miss Dorothy Paget also spent part of the considerable fortune she inherited from her maternal grandfather on Flat racers. Few justified their enormous prices, but she was leading owner in 1943 when Straight Deal won the Derby for her. Walter Nightingall trained Straight Deal but Miss Paget had several trainers, the last being Sir Gordon Richards, whose major patron Sir Michael Sobell took on the Ballymacoll Stud in Ireland which Miss Paget had bought in 1946.

MARCEL BOUSSAC (1889-1980)

Having made his fortune in the textile industry of France in the First World War, Marcel Boussac built the best stud in that country on the infleunce of the sires Tourbillon, Asterus and Pharis II. A number of his horses were trained in England, and he had his first Classic success in this country in 1940 with Djebel, but it was after the Second World War that his powerful stable reached its peak.

His subsequent Classic winners in England were Galcador (Derby), Asmena (Oaks), and Scratch II and Talma II (St Leger).

His racing fortunes went into decline after 1956, when he won
the French Derby with Philius, and it was not until 1969 that he
had his next Classic winner. Acamas won the French Derby for
him in 1978 but by that time his business was bankrupt; his
bloodstock was sold to the Aga Khan, and his stud was
purchased by Stavros Niarchos. The fall of his racing and
business interests was as spectacular as their rise.

SIR VICTOR SASSOON (1881-1961)

Racing and breeding on a lavish scale in England and India,
Sir Victor Sassoon won nine Classics between 1937 and 1960.
Between the two wars he bought several expensive horses but
it was two of his cheapest purchases—Pinza (1,500gns) and
Hard Ridden (270gns)—and two of his home-bred
horses—Crepello and St Paddy— who won the Derby for him.
Joe Lawson trained Exhibitionnist to win him the 1,000
Guineas and Oaks in 1937, while Sir Noel Murless, who
advised him on the running of his studs, trained most of his
best horses after the Second World War. He owned the Eve
Stud and Beech House Stud at Newmarket, as well as studs in
Yorkshire and Ireland.

HER MAJESTY, QUEEN ELIZABETH II (born 1926)

The Queen was extremely successful in the years immediately
after her succession, with Sir Cecil Boyd-Rochfort and Sir Noel
Murless training such as Aureole (King George VI and Queen
Elizabeth Stakes), Pall Mall (2,000 Guineas) and Carrozza
(Oaks). The Royal results went into decline in the 1960s but
were improved in the next decade when Lord Porchester
became her racing manager. The redevelopment of the Royal
Stud produced two fine Classic-winning fillies in Highclere
(1,000 Guineas and French Oaks) and Dunfermline (Oaks and
St Leger in the Queen's Silver Jubilee year).

MAJOR LIONEL HOLLIDAY (1881-1965)

Never an easy man to work for, Major Holliday changed his
trainers and jockeys with great frequency but remained one of
the most successful owner-breeders of his time, founding his
famous stud on the mare Lost Soul. He bred the sire and dam
of the Derby winner Blakeney, but never won the race
himself. Leading owner three times, he won the Oaks with
Neasham Belle, the St Leger with Hethersett and the 1,000
Guineas with Night Off—all within 14 years but each with a
different trainer. Leading breeder three times, he bred
Vaguely Noble, who in order to pay death duties was sold as a
two-year-old in 1967 for 136,000gns, the British record price
for a horse in training.

DAVID ROBINSON (born 1906)

Having entered racing in 1946 and won the 2,000 Guineas in 1955 with Our Babu, David Robinson brought a fresh aspect into racing in 1965 when he installed Bruce Hobbs as his private trainer in Newmarket. Though Hobbs stayed for only a year, Mr Robinson extended his interests so that within eight years he had more than 150 horses with two private trainers. Buying his horses and running them so as to minimise the risk of loss, he ran his stables on businesslike lines unfamiliar up to that time, with the sale of one or more horses each year as a stallion calculated to pay for the whole exercise. His chief successes were with two-year-olds and sprinters, the best being Deep Diver, So Blessed and Green God. More than once he had over 100 winners in a season, but he was leading owner for stakes only in 1969.

He studiously avoided publicity and made no secret of his low opinion of the Jockey Club, which probably explains why he was never admitted to the administration of racing. The nearest he came was when he bought Kempton Park racecourse in 1969, but after planning permission had been turned down, he sold it to the Levy Board at the price he paid. At the end of 1974 he halved his interests, and in 1979 he was no longer active as an owner.

CHARLES ENGELHARD (1917-1971)

American Charles Engelhard's colours were carried for little more than 10 years in Britain, in which time his horses won more than £532,000, with the last season before his death in 1971 his best as leading owner. His finest hour came with the Triple Crown success of Nijinsky in 1970. He completed a unique Irish Derby-English St Leger double with the brothers Ribocco and Ribero and also won the St Leger with Indiana. He had particularly high regard for the stock of Ribot. By 1979 his racing empire had been broken up.

PAUL MELLON (born 1907)

Paul Mellon's regard for England developed when he left America to become an undergraduate at Cambridge. His first interest was with steeplechasers, but his most important successes have been with Flat racers trained by Captain Peter Hastings-Bass and his successor at Kingsclere, Ian Balding. It was Balding who trained Mill Reef, the best horse to carry Mr Mellon's black and gold colours and winner of 12 races for more than £300,000, including the Derby, King George VI and Queen Elizabeth Stakes and Arc de Triomphe. Mr Mellon resisted offers to stand Mill Reef as a stallion in the United States, preferring to let him remain in England at the National Stud.

NELSON BUNKER HUNT (born 1926)

Texan Nelson Bunker Hunt was leading owner in England in 1973 and 1974 largely because of the exploits of his filly Dahlia, who won the King George VI and Queen Elizabeth Stakes in both years. Mr Hunt's first important winner in England was Golden Horus, whom he bought after he had won the Gimcrack Stakes. He was the underbidder for Vaguely Noble in 1967, but later bought a substantial share in the horse, and in 1969 he paid 110,000gns for the two-year-old Decies, who went on to win the Irish 2,000 Guineas. In 1976 he won the Derby with Empery, trained like Dahlia in France.

ROBERT SANGSTER (born 1936)

Robert Sangster took up where David Robinson left off, as the most businesslike owner in racing. The first horse in whom he had an interest was Audrey Joan, who took the Portland Handicap in 1966, and within 10 years he had developed his interests enormously, often taking on partnerships so as to secure expensive bloodstock against the wealthiest opposition. Buying chiefly in the United States, he spread his horses among several trainers, but Vincent O'Brien has been associated with most of his best horses. Leading owner for the first time in 1977, when The Minstrel won the Derby and King George VI and Queen Elizabeth Stakes, he has occupied that position three times since, and won the Derby again in 1982 with Golden Fleece.

With the help of a large team of advisers, Mr Sangster has developed huge racing and breeding interests in the United States, France and Australia, as well as Britain and Ireland, using the international market to best advantage to maximise his horses as stallions. Michael Dickinson will become his private trainer in England in late-1985, operating from a newly-bought stable at Whatcombe in Berkshire.

TRAINERS

ALEC TAYLOR (1862-1943)

Training at Manton, Alec Taylor was leading trainer 12 times, including seven times in succession from 1917 to 1923. He won 21 Classics, including the Derby with Lemberg (1910), Gay Crusader (1917) and Gainsborough (1918), as well as the Oaks eight times. Three times when he was leading trainer he set a record total for stakes won. Patient with his horses, Taylor was a bachelor who never took a holiday. He left estate worth almost £600,000 on his death.

GEORGE LAMBTON (1860-1945)

The Hon George Lambton was a noted amateur rider who was appointed private trainer to Lord Derby in 1893. For the 16th Earl of Derby he won the Oaks with Canterbury Pilgrim and Keystone II, and for the 17th Earl he won 10 Classics, including the Derby with Sansovino (1924) and Hyperion (1933). Lambton also won the 1,000 Guineas in 1917 with Diadem. Other good horses he trained included Stedfast, Phalaris, Pharos and Corrida.

Though finally relinquishing his position with Lord Derby in 1933, Lambton remained a public trainer until his death. A fine judge of a thoroughbred, he also wrote one of the best-known Turf autobiographies, 'Men and Horses I Have Known.'

PETER GILPIN (1858-1928)

Peter Gilpin began training at The Curragh in Ireland but moved to Newmarket, from where he gained his most important successes with Spearmint and Spion Kop, both Derby winners. He also trained Pretty Polly, one of the finest fillies of the century.

RICHARD DAWSON (1866-1955)

Born in Ireland and a trainer there for some years, Richard Dawson moved to Whatcombe in 1897, where he trained until his retirement in 1945 except for a brief period during the First World War when he was at Newmarket. He won the Derby and Oaks in 1916 with Fifinella, and in 10 years training for the Aga Khan saddled his Classic winners Diophon (2,000 Guineas), Blenheim (Derby) and Salmon-Trout (St Leger), as well as the brilliantly-fast Mumtaz Mahal. Dawson also won the Derby with Trigo.

FRED DARLING (1884-1953)

Fred Darling can be regarded among the top three English trainers this century, having won 19 Classics, including the Derby seven times—Captain Cuttle (1922), Manna (1925), Coronach (1926), Cameronian (1931), Bois Roussel (1938), Pont l'Eveque (1940) and Owen Tudor (1941). He also bred Pinza, whose 1953 Derby success came as Darling was on his death-bed.

Having trained briefly at Newmarket and in Ireland, Fred Darling took over the Beckhampton stable previously run by his father Sam, who trained two Derby winners. A perfectionist who ruled his stable with a rod of iron, Fred Darling also trained the unbeaten Hurry On and the brilliant but temperamental filly Sun Chariot.

FRANK BUTTERS (1878-1957)

Born in Austria, where he first began training, Frank Butters succeeded the Hon George Lambton as Lord Derby's trainer in 1926, and before his contract was terminated four years later he won for his patron the Oaks (Toboggan), 1,000 Guineas (Fair Isle) and Ascot Gold Cup (Bosworth). He also won the Oaks with Lord Durham's Beam. Following the break with Lord Derby, Butters became trainer to the Aga Khan, for whom he won nine Classics, including the Triple Crown with Bahram and the Derby with Mahmoud. In 1932 his four runners for the Aga Khan in the St Leger finished in the first five, including the winner Firdaussi. When he retired in 1949 he had trained more than 1,000 winners for stakes of over £900,000, and was leading trainer five times.

'ATTY' PERSSE (1869-1960)

Henry Seymour Persse, generally known as 'Atty', had a less successful record in the Classics than most top trainers—with three winners of the 2,000 Guineas and one of the 1,000 Guineas—but no-one had a better reputation for the art of preparing two-year-olds, especially for the occasion of their first outing. He began training in England in 1906 after four years in Ireland, and also became noted for major handicap winners, including the Kempton Park Jubilee six times. One of his Jubilee winners, Bachelor's Double, also won the Irish Derby and Royal Hunt Cup. His best horse was The Tetrarch, who was unbeaten in seven races as a two-year-old. Persse retired from training on the death of his wife in 1953.

CAPTAIN SIR CECIL BOYD-ROCHFORT (1887-1983)

Cecil Boyd-Rochfort was a success from the moment he took out a trainer's licence in 1923, the year he won the July Cup with Golden Corn. He remained so until handing over to his stepson Henry Cecil in 1968, the year he was knighted. Boyd-Rochfort was particularly successful with stayers, and of his 13 Classic winners, six were in the St Leger, while he won the Ascot Gold Cup three times and the Goodwood Cup six times.

Appointed trainer to King George VI in 1943, he held the Royal position until his retirement. Among the good horses he trained for the Queen were Aureole, Doutelle, Pall Mall, Almeria and Above Suspicion. Meld, winner of three Classics, and Alcide, winner of the King George VI and Queen Elizabeth Stakes were among the best horses he trained.

SIR NOEL MURLESS (born 1910)

Born in Cheshire and a trainer first in Yorkshire with moderate horses, Noel Murless moved south in 1947 when invited to succeed Fred Darling at Beckhampton. He stayed there for five years before moving to Newmarket, where he became the top trainer of his day. Nine times leading trainer, he set record stakes totals in 1957, 1959 and 1967, and when he retired at the end of 1976 he had won 19 Classics, including the Derby with Crepello (1957), St Paddy (1960) and Royal Palace (1967).

A great stableman, Murless was a master at bringing out his runners fit to do themselves justice without being got ready on the racecourse. He always set his sights on the best races but put the interests of his horses first. He was knighted in June 1977 and elected to the Jockey Club the following month.

CAPT CHARLES ELSEY (1882-1966)

Year after year Charles Elsey sent out more winners from his Malton stable than any other trainer in the North and on his retirement in 1961 had trained 1,548 winners worth almost £800,000. He was leading trainer in 1956, the year he won the 1,000 Guineas with Honeylight. He won five other Classics but never the Derby. He was particularly successful in major handicaps, and won the Ebor, Northumberland Plate and Lincoln three times.

MAJOR DICK HERN (born 1921)

Dick Hern trained Hethersett to win the St Leger for Major Lionel Holliday in 1962, but at the end of that season, when he was leading trainer for the first time, he gave up the appointment to succeed RJ Colling at West Ilsley. Since then his has become one of the most powerful stables in the country, with Royal patronage, and Hern has become one of the best trainers of his time.

He won the Derby in successive years with Troy and Henbit, and has won the St Leger a further four times, including with Dunfermline, winner of the Oaks. Leading trainer four times, his other top horses have included Brigadier Gerard, who was beaten only once in 18 races, and Highclere, who gave the Queen a Classic success abroad when winning the French Oaks.

PADDY PRENDERGAST (1909-80)

Paddy Prendergast was the first Irish-based trainer to have consistent success in England after the Second World War, and was leading trainer for three consecutive years beginning 1963. His runners were particularly feared at Chester and York, but most especially at Royal Ascot, where he won the Coventry Stakes six times from 1953 to 1969. In his years as leading trainer in England he won the Oaks (Noblesse), St Leger (Ragusa) and 1,000 Guineas (Pourparler), as well as the Eclipse Stakes with Khalkis and Ragusa, and the King George VI and Queen Elizabeth Stakes with Ragusa and Meadow

Court. His first Classic success had been in the 2,000 Guineas with Martial (1960).

VINCENT O'BRIEN (born 1917)

Armed with some of the wealthiest owners in the world, many of them from the United States, and using horses bred mainly in America, Vincent O'Brien took Paddy Prendergast's achievements a stage further and higher. Having had considerable success as a National Hunt trainer, including winning the Grand National three times, the Cheltenham Gold Cup four times and the Champion Hurdle three times, O'Brien turned to the Flat and was leading trainer in Britain for the first time in 1966, the year that Glad Rags won the 1,000 Guineas and Valoris the Oaks.

O'Brien had already won the Derby in 1962 with Larkspur, and further successes have come with Sir Ivor (1968), Nijinsky (the Triple Crown winner of 1970), Roberto (1972), The Minstrel (1977) and Golden Fleece (1982). The Minstrel's success enabled O'Brien to become leading trainer in Britain for the second time. To add to his genius O'Brien employed Lester Piggott in most of his major successes until 1981, when Pat Eddery was signed as Robert Sangster's jockey. Eddery began where Piggott left off, and in his first three years with O'Brien they won the Irish 2,000 Guineas (Kings Lake), Derby (Golden Fleece), Benson and Hedges Gold Cup (Assert and Caerleon), 2,000 Guineas (Lomond), French Derby (Caerleon) and Eclipse Stakes (Solford). When El Gran Senor won the 1983 Dewhurst Stakes it gave O'Brien his seventh winner of the race in 15 years.

PETER WALWYN (born 1933)

Having held a licence on behalf of his cousin Mrs Johnson Houghton for six years, Peter Walwyn began on his own account at Lambourn in 1961. Gaining an early reputation for handling fillies, he won the 1,000 Guineas in 1970 with Humble Duty and the Oaks in 1974 with Polygamy before in 1975 he won the Derby with Grundy, who also took the King George VI and Queen Elizabeth after an epic race against Bustino.

Walwyn was leading trainer for the first time in 1974, and the following year he repeated the feat with 120 winners, the highest in the 20th century. Walwyn, whose chief disappointments have centred round the twice-disqualified Ascot Gold Cup 'winner' Rock Roi, took on Pat Eddery as stable jockey as soon as he finished his apprenticeship.

HENRY CECIL (born 1943)

Stepson of Sir Cecil Boyd-Rochfort and married to Noel Murless's daughter, Henry Cecil was the same immediate success as a trainer that his stepfather had been 46 years earlier, in his first season winning the 1969 Eclipse Stakes with Wolver Hollow. He won his first Classic in 1973 with Cloonagh (Irish 1,000 Guineas) and his first English Classic two years later with Bolkonski (2,000 Guineas). In 1976 he was leading trainer for the first time, and has attained the position three times since, with record earnings of £872,614 in 1982 and a 20th century record of 128 winners in 1979.

A meticulous planner who prefers to be at home with his horses rather than be seen unnecessarily on the racecourse, Cecil rarely runs his horses abroad and has shown himself adept with all types of horses from sprinters to stayers, and two-year-olds to seniors.

JOCKEYS

MORNINGTON CANNON (1873-1962)

'Morny' Cannon was an expert at riding a waiting race. He won six Classics, including the Triple Crown in 1899 on Flying Fox, and was champion jockey six times.

DANNY MAHER (1881-1916)

Along with Tod Sloan, who rode more than 250 winners from fewer than 1,000 rides in Britain, and the Rieff brothers, Danny Maher spearheaded the appearance of American jockeys that was a characteristic of the early years of the 20th century. Maher, a champion jockey in America, occupied the same position in Britain in 1908 and 1913. He rode three Derby winners: Rock Sand (1903), Cicero (1905) and Spearmint (1906), as well as the winners of six other Classics. Excessive wasting and high living took its toll on his health, already weakened by tuberculosis, and he was a sick man when he returned to America in 1914.

FRANK WOOTTON (1894-1940)

Only Lester Piggott can match Frank Wootton's youthful success this century. From his first winner at the age of 13 to the time he was forced to give up Flat racing because of increasing weight seven years later, Wootton rode 882 winners, including being champion jockey at the age of 16. He won the Oaks on Perola (1909) and the St Leger on Swynford (1910), and was champion jockey in four successive seasons from 1909. After the First World War he rode over hurdles and later turned to training before he returned to his native Australia in 1933.

STEVE DONOGHUE (1884-1945)

The most famous and popular jockey of his day, Steve
Donoghue was champion 10 years running, from 1914 to 1923,
sharing the title with Charlie Elliott on the last occasion. It was
in France that he rode his first winner, in 1905, and he did not
return to England until 1911, after a spell in Ireland between.
He was first associated with 'Atty' Persse's stable, and rode
The Tetrarch, but the height of his career was in the first half of
the 1920s.

The cry 'Come on Steve' became nationally known as he
went about winning 14 Classics, including the Derby on
Pommern (1915), Gay Crusader (1917), Humorist (1921),
Captain Cuttle (1922), Papyrus (1923) and Manna (1925). He
also won the Irish Derby four times and the Grand Prix de Paris
twice, and was associated with the equally popular Brown
Jack. His last important success was at the age of 52, on the
1937 Oaks winner Exhibitionnist, and when he retired that

Steve Donoghue, winner of 14 Classics.

year he completed a record of never having been in trouble with the stewards. A brilliant horseman and a master of the track at Epsom, he was held in the highest esteem by his colleagues and the public alike.

TOMMY WESTON (1903-1981)

Tommy Weston, stable jockey to Lord Derby from 1924 to 1934, was Hyperion's rider in winning the Derby and St Leger, though he regarded Sansovino, the 1924 Derby winner, as the best horse he rode. Champion jockey in 1926, he was a leading lightweight jockey before becoming contracted to Lord Derby and continued in the top flight when that arrangement was ended unexpectedly. He won the Oaks in 1936 on Lovely Rosa, and having served in the Royal Navy in the Second World War, resumed riding and won his 11th Classic on Happy Knight in the 2,000 Guineas in 1946. He retired from riding in 1950.

SIR GORDON RICHARDS (born 1904)

Determination and a reputation for total honesty made Gordon Richards the favourite jockey for millions of small punters; vigorous finishing in an unmistakable but unorthodox style and an unquenchable will to win made him the most successful jockey this century, with 4,870 winners from 21,843 mounts between 1920 and 1954. Only Lester Piggott is mentioned in the same breath when arguments take place about the best jockey.

One of 12 children, he rode his first winner in 1921 and in his initial season out of his apprenticeship, 1925, he became champion jockey for the first time with 118 winners. He was champion 26 times, and from 1925 to 1953 only Tommy Weston (1926), Freddy Fox (1930) and Harry Wragg (1941) halted his run, though in 1926 he did not ride after May because of illness and in 1941 he was out from the same month with a broken leg. He broke Fred Archer's record of 246 winners in a season, set in 1885, with 259 winners in 1933, the year he rode 12 consecutive winners (one at Nottingham and 11 at a two-day Chepstow fixture when his last ride was beaten at long odds-on), and bettered that in 1947 with 269 winners.

Riding originally for Martin Hartigan, to whom he was apprenticed, and Capt T Hogg, he became stable jockey to Fred Darling in 1932, and remained with Darling's successor, Noel Murless, when he moved to Newmarket in 1952. Murless did not have a runner in the Derby the following year and Richards was left to accept the ride on Pinza for Norman Bertie, who had been Darling's travelling head lad. Pinza, bred by Darling, gave Richards his first and only Derby success, which to that time had been the sole blemish on his career after 13 other Classic successes.

Two falls in 1954 ended Richards's riding career, though he had already decided that would be his final season, and he began training at Darling's old yard at Beckhampton. He moved to Ogbourne Maisey in 1955 and to Whitsbury in 1965, but was forced to find new stables in 1969. When no suitable property came up he retired to manage the horses owned by two of his patrons, Sir Michael Sobell and Lady Beaverbrook. Pipe of Peace (third in the 2,000 Guineas and Derby), Court Harwell (second in the St Leger) and Reform (winner of the Champion Stakes) were the best horses he trained.

HARRY WRAGG (born 1902)

Harry Wragg, whose brothers Arthur and Sam were also jockeys, was one of the most intelligent jockeys of his day, and his patient tactics earned him the nickname 'The Head Waiter'. Apprenticed to RW Colling at Newmarket, Harry Wragg rode his first winner in 1919 and soon had several important retainers, including for Mr SB Joel. He won his first Classic in 1928, on Felstead in the Derby, and his last in 1946, on Steady Aim in the Oaks, in the year he retired from riding. His 13 Classic winners included two more in the Derby, Blenheim (1930) and Watling Street (1942). Watling Street was one of six Classic winners he rode for Lord Derby in the space of four seasons.

Wragg began training at Newmarket in 1947 having been champion jockey only once, in 1941, the year Gordon Richards broke a leg. One of the few trainers to time horses on the gallops, he was also an innovator in weighing his horses regularly, and was one of the first in recent times to send horses abroad to race. The Oaks was the only Classic to elude him as a trainer, and having won the Derby with Psidium in 1961, he completed his total of Classic successes with On the House (1,000 Guineas) in his last season, 1982. He handed over his stable to his son Geoffrey, who won the Derby in 1983 with Teenoso in his first season.

CHARLIE SMIRKE (born 1906)

Charlie Smirke was the archetypal Cockney, extrovert and never afraid to speak his mind but confident when it mattered most. He was never champion jockey, upset several owners by his attitude, and was once warned off by the Jockey Club, though perhaps unfairly, but he remained the man for the big occasion. He was associated with the Aga Khan on and off for 30 years and rode six of his 11 Classic winners for that owner, including Mahmoud (1936) and Tulyar (1952) in the Derby. His other Derby successes were on Windsor Lad (1934) and Hard Ridden (1958), the latter being one of only three winners from 19 rides in his penultimate season.

DOUG SMITH (born 1917)

Apprenticed like his elder brother Eph to Major FB Sneyd,
Doug Smith was champion jockey five times in the six years
immediately after Gordon Richards's retirement, with totals
that varied between 129 and 168. His Classic successes came
in the 2,000 and 1,000 Guineas, which he won twice each, but
he was particularly effective in staying races, and he won the
Cesarewitch six times and the Doncaster Cup seven times.
Associated with the Middleham trainer Harry Peacock for
more than 20 years, he was first jockey to Frank Butters and for
four years was the Royal jockey until retained by Lord Derby,
for whom he was unlucky in the Derby on Swallow Tail, being
beaten two heads into third place behind Nimbus after being
bumped at the distance.

In the last 12 years of his riding career he was also
associated with Geoffrey Brooke's stable, for whom he won
several important two-year-old races, including the Coventry
Stakes, Gimcrack Stakes, Champagne Stakes and Middle Park
Stakes twice each. Brooke retired in 1967, when Smith gave
up riding to run a public stable at Newmarket and while also
training privately for Lord Rosebery he had his most important
success in the Oaks with Sleeping Partner in 1969. He retired
from training in 1979.

SCOBIE BREASLEY (born 1914)

Arthur Edward Breasley, known as 'Scobie', was the best of
the Australian jockeys who came to Britain from 1950, the year
he joined Noel Cannon's stable after having made his name
as a champion jockey in Australia. He rode four Classic

Scobie Breasley left, and Lester Piggott pictured in 1964

winners, including the Derby for the first time at the age of 50 on Santa Claus in 1964 and again two years later on Charlottown, and was champion jockey four times. A brilliant judge of pace, Breasley was also adept on two-year-olds and highly-strung fillies who responded to his sympathetic style. He rode for Sir Gordon Richards from 1956 until his retirement at the end of 1967. A trainer at Epsom, Chantilly and New York, chiefly for Mr Ravi Tikkoo, he had his biggest success with Steel Pulse in the Irish Sweeps Derby, and after a short spell back in England at Epsom, retired from training in 1980.

LESTER PIGGOTT (born 1935)

Outstandingly successful as a boy, Lester Piggott became a firm favourite with the public despite his brushes with authority and an apparent dislike of publicity—or perhaps because of these qualities. He rode his first winner at the age of 12, was suspended by the Jockey Club for the first time, for four weeks, two years later, and almost won his first Derby at the age of 16 in 1952 on Gay Time, who was beaten less than a length by Tulyar. He did win the Derby in 1954 on Never Say Die, and a fortnight later was suspended for six months after riding a rough race on the same horse at Royal Ascot.

Piggott was ordered to spend the period of his suspension with a trainer other than his father, and Jack Jarvis took on the job that may be said to have rescued the career of the finest jockey since Gordon Richards. In 1955 Piggott succeeded Richards as stable jockey to Noel Murless and in 12 years they formed a formidable partnership, winning seven Classics, including the Derby with Crepello (1957) and St Paddy (1960). In 1966 the association broke up when Piggott took the ride on Valoris in the Oaks rather than a runner from the Murless stable. Valoris won, and though Piggott rode for Murless on occasions, this marked the beginning of his time as a freelance and his association with Vincent O'Brien, trainer of Valoris. For O'Brien he won the Derby on Sir Ivor (1968), Nijinsky (1970), Roberto (1972) and The Minstrel (1977). Empery (1976) and Teenoso (1983) complete Piggott's all-time record of nine Derby winners, and his total of 26 Classic winners is five ahead of Fred Archer, two ahead of Jem Robinson, and only one behind the record-holder Frank Buckle.

Leading apprentice in 1950 and 1951, Piggott was champion senior jockey for the first time in 1960, and has since occupied the position on 10 occasions, including eight in a row from 1964 to 1971. His last two occasions as champion jockey, 1981 and 1982, came after signing as stable jockey to Henry Cecil. Always mindful that his natural weight is not that of a Flat-race jockey, Piggott has the reputation of being a shrewd businessman, and when he decides the time has come to retire from riding he will have a number of training establishments in Newmarket to choose as his base.

WILLIE CARSON (born 1942)

Willie Carson was 20 before he rode his first winner and it was another nine years before he rode 100 winners in a season for the first time. In 1972 he rode his first Classic winner, High Top in the 2,000 Guineas, and was champion jockey for the first time, with 132 winners. He has since been champion jockey a further four times.

He rode principally for Bernard van Cutsem, Barry Hills and Clive Brittain before his big break came in 1977, when he succeeded Joe Mercer as first jockey to Dick Hern. In his first season there he won the Oaks and St Leger on the Queen's Dunfermline; he won the Derby for the stable on Troy (1979) and Henbit (1980), and in 1980 completed the Epsom Classic double on Bireme. He missed three months of the season in 1981 after a bad fall, but the experience did not affect his confidence and chirpy nature and he regained his title as champion jockey in 1983, when he won the Oaks on Sun Princess, who also finished second in the Arc de Triomphe.

PAT EDDERY (born 1952)

Pat Eddery gave notice of his outstanding promise in 1970, 16 months after riding his first winner, when as an apprentice with 'Frenchie' Nicholson he rode five winners in seven rides at a Haydock Park meeting. Leading apprentice in 1971, he ended his apprenticeship the following year and became retained by Peter Walwyn, for whom he gained his first Classic success on Polygamy in the Oaks in 1974. That was also the first of four successive years he was champion jockey, and he also won the Derby for the first time for the stable on Grundy in 1975. In 1980 Eddery ended his association with Walwyn to be retained by Vincent O'Brien and his principal patron Robert Sangster, for whom he won the Derby on Golden Fleece in 1982, the year he was also champion jockey in his native

Willie Carson, champion jockey five times.

Ireland for the first time despite being based in England. His other major wins for O'Brien have been in the Irish 2,000 Guineas (Kings Lake), Benson and Hedges Gold Cup (Assert and Caerleon), 2,000 Guineas (Lomond), French Derby (Caerleon) and Eclipse Stakes (Solford), while he won the Arc de Triomphe in 1980 for Mr Sangster on Detroit.

HORSES

SCEPTRE (1899)

b f Persimmon - Ornament (Bend Or)

Sceptre had the unique distinction of winning four of the five Classics—the 2,000 Guineas in record time, the 1,000 Guineas two days later, the Oaks two days after finishing fourth in the Derby on an interrupted preparation, and the St Leger. In 1902 she also ran in the Grand Prix de Paris, twice at Royal Ascot and in the Park Hill Stakes two days after the St Leger over the same distance. Owned and trained by Robert Sievier, she failed to make her reserve at the December Sales in 1902, but after failing to land a gamble in the following year's Lincoln, she was sold for £25,000. She went on racing until the age of five and at stud was responsible for a family that included four Derby seconds between 1919 and 1924 as well as the Classic winners Craig an Eran, Taboun, Match III, Relko, Reliance II and Full Dress II.

PERSIMMON (1893)

b c St Simon - Perdita II (Hampton)

Winner of the Coventry Stakes as a two-year-old first time out, Persimmon went on to win the Derby, St Leger and Ascot Gold Cup. Leading sire four times between 1902 and 1912, Persimmon was the best son of St Simon, a stallion of the highest order and leading sire nine times. Persimmon's produce included Sceptre and Prince Palatine (winner of the Ascot Gold Cup twice).

PRETTY POLLY (1901)

ch f Gallinule - Admiration (Saraband)

Pretty Polly raced for four seasons and won all but two of her 24 races, including the 1,000 Guineas, Oaks, St Leger, Coronation Cup and Champion Stakes. She bred only four winners but became a first-class influence since her descendants include two Derby winners in St Paddy and Psidium, as well as Donatello II, Premonition and Brigadier Gerard.

POLYMELUS (1902)

b c Cyllene - Maid Marian (Hampton)

During four years in training Polymelus won races valued at £16,725 and though thought to be best at around a mile and a quarter he finished second in the Derby and third in the St Leger. He was champion sire five times, a record that only Hyperion has beaten in the 20th century, and his produce included the Derby winners Pommern, Fifinella and Humorist. He owes his influence on modern pedigrees to his son, the handicapper Phalaris.

BAYARDO (1906)

b c Bay Ronald - Rosedrop (St Frusquin)

Bayardo won 22 of his 25 races, including the St Leger and Ascot Gold Cup. Despite his early death at the age of 11, he was an unqualified success at stud, where he sired the Triple Crown winners Gay Crusader and Gainsborough, and the Oaks winner Bayuda. Bayardo was champion sire in 1917 and 1918.

SON-IN-LAW (1911)

br c Dark Ronald - Mother-in-Law (Matchmaker)

Though considerably below Classic standard, Son-in-Law was a formidable stayer who won eight races including the Cesarewitch, Jockey Club Cup twice and Goodwood Cup. Champion sire twice, he got only one Classic winner, Straitlace (Oaks), and only one Derby winner, Pont l'Eveque, traces to him in the direct male line. But Son-in-Law can be counted among the most important influences in 20th century pedigrees, for he got many top-class horses after his own style of a stout-hearted stayer. Foxlaw, Bosworth and Trimdon were Ascot Gold Cup winners by Son-in-Law, while Marsyas (by Trimdon) won the French Gold Cup four times.

THE TETRARCH (1911)

gr c Roi Herode - Vahren (Bona Vista)

So unusual in looks that he was called 'The Spotted Wonder', The Tetrarch was also outstanding for his tremendous speed, which took him unbeaten through seven races as a two-year-old. He never raced again, as he was injured when being prepared for the Derby. His stud career lasted until his death in 1935 but he was sterile for the last 10 years of his life and in the previous 10 years he had only 130 foals. Despite his lack of foals, The Tetrarch sired 80 winners, four of them won in the Classics including three in the St Leger — Polemarch, Caligula and Salmon-Trout. Champion sire in 1919, The Tetrarch also sired Tetratema, himself a champion sire after winning the 2,000 Guineas, and the brilliant Mumtaz Mahal.

PHALARIS (1913)

br c Polymelus - Bromus (Sainfoin)

Phalaris as a racehorse proved no better than a decent handicapper, winning 15 races, but from his 12 years at stud he achieved astonishing success and came to exert an influence second to none on modern pedigrees. Champion sire twice, he got the brothers Pharos and Fairway, the Derby winner Manna, the 2,000 Guineas winner Colorado and the 1,000 Guineas winner Fair Isle.

BLANDFORD (1919)

br c Swynford - Blanche (White Eagle)

Fortunate to survive pneumonia as a foal and never an easy horse to train, Blandford had only four races, winning three and being beaten a short head in the other. Leg trouble forced him to be retired to stud, and in 1935, the year he died, he was champion sire in both Britain and France. Champion sire on two other occasions, he got the Derby winners Trigo, Blenheim, Windsor Lad and Bahram. In France he was responsible for Brantome, winner of the French 2,000 Guineas and St Leger.

BROWN JACK (1924)

br g Jackdaw - Querquidella (Kroonstad)

Brown Jack was a most popular stayer who won 18 races for £21,646 on the Flat, and seven over hurdles. Bred in Ireland, where he was gelded before he ran, he had his first race in England over hurdles and won the Champion Hurdle before Steve Donoghue suggested to his owner that he should be trained for the Flat. Donoghue became his regular rider and Brown Jack gained fame by winning the Queen Alexandra Stakes over two and threequarter miles at Royal Ascot six years in a row. He also won the Chester Cup, Ascot Stakes, Goodwood Cup and Ebor Handicap.

FAIRWAY (1925)

b c Phalaris - Scapa Flow (Chaucer)

Bred by Lord Derby and winner of 12 races including the St Leger, Fairway was champion sire four times to the once of his brother Pharos (1920), who stood for three years in England before being sent to·France. Fairway's sons included the Derby

winners Blue Peter and Watling Street, and the champion sire
Fair Trial, from whom a notable sire line has emerged. A
similarly important sire line emanated from Pharos, the sire of
Pharis II, the French Derby winner and a champion sire in
France, and the Italian-bred Nearco. The best winners bred by
Pharos in England were Cameronian (2,000 Guineas and
Derby) and Firdaussi (St Leger).

HYPERION (1930)

ch c Gainsborough - Selene (Chaucer)

Hyperion proved the exception to the rule that a good big 'un
will always beat a good little 'un, as he overcame his lack of
inches to win the Derby and St Leger before becoming an
outstanding influence at stud. Champion sire six times, he got
only one Derby winner in Owen Tudor but his daughter Sun
Chariot won the 1,000 Guineas, Oaks and St Leger while
Godiva, Sun Castle, Hycilla, Sunstream and Hypericum also
won Classics. He also sired the smart racer Aureole, who
became twice champion sire, while his sons Alibhai, Khaled
and Heliopolis were very successful in the United States.
Hyperion's influence can now be seen worldwide.

NEARCO (1935)

br c Pharos - Nogara (Havresac II)

A magnificent individual and a smart racehorse bred in Italy
by Federico Tesio, Nearco won the Italian Derby by a distance
and after beating the English and French Derby winners in the
Grand Prix de Paris was bought to stand at stud in Newmarket,
where he remained until his death in 1957. Nearco had his
first Derby-winning son in 1945, with Dante, and in the
following 38 years a total of 12 Derby winners traced to
Nearco in the male line. This remarkable incidence is an
indication of his influence on top-class thoroughbred
breeding, achieved largely through the exploits of his sons
Nasrullah, Royal Charger and Mossborough.

BLUE PETER (1936)

ch c Fairway - Fancy Free (Stefan the Great)

But for the intervention of the Second World War, Blue Peter
would probably have been a Triple Crown winner, for he won
the 2,000 Guineas, Derby and Eclipse Stakes well enough to
suggest he would prove too good for the French-trained Pharis
II in the St Leger. This handsome horse was retired to stud as a
four-year-old, got two Ascot Gold Cup winners in Ocean Swell
(also won the Derby) and Botticelli but in view of his own
ability was regarded as slightly disappointing as a stallion.

NASRULLAH (1940)

b c Nearco - Singing Grass (War Admiral)

Bred in Ireland by the Aga Khan, for whom he won five races during wartime-restricted racing at Newmarket, Nasrullah was very temperamental but from first crop to last as a stallion he was an outstanding success. After standing for one season in England, he was sold to stand in Ireland and finally went to America in 1950. Though champion sire in Britain only once, he has become one of the most influential stallions of the age, especially through his sons born in the United States, where he was leading sire five times. Nashua, Bold Ruler and Never Bend (sire of Mill Reef) are strong influences among his American sons, while the best of those standing in Britain have been Red God, Grey Sovereign and Princely Gift. Never Say Die, the Derby winner, was Nasrullah's best produce to race in Britain.

TUDOR MINSTREL (1944)

br c Owen Tudor - Sansonnet (Sansovino)

Tudor Minstrel was a brilliantly fast horse who went through his two-year-old career unbeaten, won the 2,000 Guineas by eight lengths but failed to stay the distance when fourth to Pearl Diver in the Derby. His eight victories were gained up to a mile, and though he sired the Kentucky Derby winner Tomy Lee, his chief successes at stud in England were the speedy two-year-olds Sing Sing and Tudor Melody. Tudor Minstrel was exported to the United States in 1959 and ended his stud duties in 1970.

MELD (1952)

b f Alycidon - Daily Double (Fair Trial)

There have been few better staying fillies this century than Meld, who won the 1,000 Guineas, Oaks, Coronation Stakes and St Leger as a three-year-old. She won the St Leger by less than a length but that night was found to be running a temperature. A good-looking filly whose five wins were worth £43,051, she bred the Derby winner Charlottown but several of her offspring lacked her courage. Her unraced son Mellay (by Never Say Die) was highly successful at stud in New Zealand. Meld died in 1983.

RIBOT (1952)

b c Tenerani - Romanella (El Greco)

Ribot was the last great horse bred by Federico Tesio, who did not live to see him run. He was unbeaten in 16 races from five furlongs to 15 furlongs on going ranging from hard to heavy, and his three races outside Italy confirmed his high class. He won the Arc de Triomphe twice and the King George VI and Queen Elizabeth Stakes. He spent his first season at stud in England, the next three in Italy and the rest of his life until his death in 1972 in the United States. His stock were not precocious and it was to his advantage that owners such as Charles Engelhard and patrons of Vincent O'Brien's stable were prepared to buy Ribot produce in America to race in Britain and Ireland. After producing the Arc de Triomphe winners Molvedo and Prince Royal II, as well as Ragusa, among his European crops, Ribot was responsible for the Preakness Stakes winner Tom Rolfe, the brothers Ribocco and Ribero, the Oaks winner Long Look, and the St Leger winner Boucher. So many sons of Ribot have done well throughout the world that it will be a surprise if he is not a powerful influence on breeding for a considerable time.

PETITE ETOILE (1956)

gr f Petition - Star of Iran (Bois Roussel)

Petite Etoile's lack of success at stud has been in sharp contrast to her brilliant racing career, in which she won 14 races for £72,626, including the 1,000 Guineas, Oaks, Sussex Stakes and Champion Stakes at three years, and Coronation Cup at four and five years. She might also have won the King George VI and Queen Elizabeth Stakes, instead of being beaten half a length by Aggressor, if Lester Piggott, her regular rider, had not ridden a poor race.

SEA-BIRD II (1962)

ch c Dan Cupid - Sicalade (Sicambre)

Sea-Bird II has claims to be regarded the best post-war Derby winner. Trained in France, he was beaten only once in eight

Sea Bird II, after winning the 1965 Derby.

races and came into his own as a three-year-old by winning the Derby by an easy two lengths and the strongly-contested Arc de Triomphe by six lengths. He was leased to stand his first five years at stud in the United States; the lease was extended for a further two years, but on his return to France for the 1973 season he contracted colic and died. He had seven crops to represent him and his best son, Gyr, who finished second to Nijinsky in the Derby, came from the first. Sea-Bird's best produce was Allez France.

VAGUELY NOBLE (1965)

b c Vienna - Noble Lassie (Nearco)

The gamble that Californian plastic surgeon Dr Robert Franklyn took when he paid 136,000gns for Vaguely Noble as a back-end two-year-old with no classic engagements came off handsomely. He earned almost his purchase price with four wins in France as a three-year-old, including the Arc de Triomphe, and was retired to stud in the United States with a valuation of £2 million. Thanks to support from Nelson Bunker Hunt, who took a half-share in him for his racing career in France, Vaguely Noble had the good fortune that several of his produce were raced in Europe, where late-maturing stock would be better suited by the conditions. Dahlia, who won top-class races in five countries, was from Vaguely Noble's first crop; Mississippian, the French 2,000 Guineas winner, was in the second; Nobiliary, the Washington International winner, in the third, and Empery, the Derby winner, in the fourth.

NIJINSKY (1967)

b c Northern Dancer - Flaming Page (Bull Page)

The first Canadian-bred horse to win the Derby, Nijinsky was also the first to complete the Triple Crown since Bahram in 1935. He won 11 races, and as well as the English Classics won the Irish Sweeps Derby and the King George VI and Queen Elizabeth Stakes. His only defeats came on his last two outings when he was second in the Arc de Triomphe and Champion Stakes. Retired to stud in Kentucky, he was an instant success, with the Classic winners Green Dancer (French 2,000 Guineas) and Caucasus (Irish St Leger) in his first crop. Niniski (Irish and French St Legers) and Kings Lake (Irish 2,000 Guineas) followed as Nijinsky's next Classic winners, while Ile de Bourbon won the King George VI and Queen Elizabeth Stakes. In 1982 Nijinsky had his first winner of an English Classic, Golden Fleece, who achieved the rare distinction of becoming a Derby winner sired by a Derby winner. Along with his own sire Northern Dancer, Nijinsky is the hottest property on the thoroughbred markets of the world.

MILL REEF (1968)

b c Never Bend - Milan Mill (Princequillo)

A complicated fracture of the near foreleg ended Mill Reef's racing career as a four-year-old after 12 wins and two seconds from his 14 races, including victories in the Derby, Eclipse Stakes, King George VI and Queen Elizabeth Stakes, and Arc de Triomphe. Except that he was a valuable stallion proposition and expense was of secondary importance, Mill Reef might have been put down. Instead he was saved and sent to the National Stud at Newmarket to become the most expensive stallion in England. From his first full crop he sired the Derby winner Shirley Heights and the French Derby winner Acamas, with the result that in 1978 Mill Reef was champion sire. Fairy Footsteps (1,000 Guineas), Glint of Gold (Italian Derby) and his brother Diamond Shoal (Grand Prix de Saint-Cloud) have since helped to prove Mill Reef's worth.

BRIGADIER GERARD (1968)

b c Queen's Hussar - La Paiva (Prince Chevalier)

Though Brigadier Gerard won 15 races in a row and came back from his one defeat in the Benson and Hedges Gold Cup to win his last two races, there was a disappointing angle to his career in that a meeting with Mill Reef over middle-distances did not take place. On their only encounter, over a mile in the 2,000 Guineas, Brigadier Gerard beat Mill Reef three lengths into second place. Brigadier Gerard won the Champion Stakes as a three-year-old and completed the double the following year with a performance that totally restored his fine reputation after his single defeat by Roberto at York. Retired to stand at stud in Newmarket, Brigadier Gerard has not been a success to compare with Mill Reef, his best winners being Light Cavalry (St Leger) and Vayrann (Champion Stakes).

ALLEZ FRANCE (1970)

b f Sea-Bird II - Priceless Gem (Hail to Reason)

Bred in the United States and bought there by Daniel Wildenstein to race in France, Allez France developed a remarkable rivalry with another high-class, American-bred filly, Dahlia. Six times Allez France met Dahlia, and six times she finished in front, yet Allez France won less prize money than her rival. Allez France, who had blistering finishing pace, won 13 races from 21 outings in four seasons, her chief victories coming in the Arc de Triomphe, French Oaks and French 1,000 Guineas. She also ran second in another Arc, and twice second in the Champion Stakes at Newmarket, on neither occasion showing the top form that European racegoers knew was possible.

DAHLIA (1970)

ch f Vaguely Noble - Charming Alibi (Honeys Alibi)

Like her great rival Allez France, Dahlia raced for four seasons, and is credited with winning more prize money than that other fine French-trained filly for a record among stakes winners trained in Europe. Dahlia was not so powerful as Allez France but she kept her form better when travelling outside France and won in five different countries. She won the King George VI and Queen Elizabeth Stakes twice, the Benson and Hedges Gold Cup twice, the Irish Oaks, Washington International and Canadian International Championship among her 15 victories. She was also placed 15 times.

SHERGAR (1978)

b c Great Nephew - Sharmeen (Val de Loir)

For the first time since 1952 the colours of the Aga Khan were carried to success in the Derby when Shergar won in 1981. What is more he established a 10-length margin that had not been bettered in the history of the race. He was unbeaten as a three-year-old until finishing fourth in the St Leger, after which he was retired to his owner's Ballymany Stud in Ireland at a valuation of £10 million, a record for a stallion to stand at stud in Europe. He covered his first crop of mares in 1982, but a few days before the 1983 covering season was due to start he was stolen. At the time of writing he is still missing.

Shergar, won the Derby in 1981 by a record ten length margin.

CHAMPION JOCKEYS

Year	Jockey		Year	Jockey	
1846	E Flatman	81	1892	M Cannon	182
1847	E Flatman	89	1893	T Loates	222
1848	E Flatman	104	1894	M Cannon	167
1849	E Flatman	94	1895	M Cannon	184
1850	E Flatman	88	1896	M Cannon	164
1851	E Flatman	78	1897	M Cannon	145
1852	E Flatman	92	1898	O Madden	161
1853	J Wells	86	1899	S Loates	160
1854	J Wells	82	1900	L Reiff	143
1855	G Fordham	70	1901	O Madden	130
1856	G Fordham	108	1902	W Lane	170
1857	G Fordham	84	1903	O Madden	154
1858	G Fordham	91	1904	O Madden	161
1859	G Fordham	118	1905	E Wheatley	124
1860	G Fordham	146	1906	W Higgs	149
1861	G Fordham	106	1907	W Higgs	146
1862	G Fordham	166	1908	D Maher	139
1863	G Fordham	103	1909	F Wootton	165
1864	J Grimshaw	164	1910	F Wootton	137
1865	G Fordham	142	1911	F Wootton	187
1866	S Kenyon	123	1912	F Wootton	118
1867	G Fordham	143	1913	D Maher	115
1868	G Fordham	110	1914	S Donoghue	129
1869	G Fordham	95	1915	S Donoghue	62
1870	W Grey	76	1916	S Donoghue	43
1870	C Maidment	76	1917	S Donoghue	42
1871	G Fordham	86	1918	S Donoghue	66
1871	C Maidment	86	1919	S Donoghue	129
1872	T Cannon	87	1920	S Donoghue	143
1873	H Constable	110	1921	S Donoghue	141
1874	F Archer	147	1922	S Donoghue	102
1875	F Archer	172	1923	S Donoghue	89
1876	F Archer	207	1923	C Elliott	89
1877	F Archer	218	1924	C Elliott	106
1878	F Archer	229	1925	G Richards	118
1879	F Archer	197	1926	T Weston	95
1880	F Archer	120	1927	G Richards	164
1881	F Archer	220	1928	G Richards	148
1882	F Archer	210	1929	G Richards	135
1883	F Archer	232	1930	F Fox	129
1884	F Archer	241	1931	G Richards	145
1885	F Archer	246	1932	G Richards	190
1886	F Archer	170	1933	G Richards	259
1887	C Wood	151	1934	G Richards	212
1888	F Barrett	108	1935	G Richards	217
1889	T Loates	167	1936	G Richards	174
1890	T Loates	147	1937	G Richards	216
1891	M Cannon	137	1938	G Richards	206

Year	Jockey	Wins	Year	Jockey	Wins
1939	G Richards	155	1962	A Breasley	179
1940	G Richards	68	1963	A Breasley	176
1941	H Wragg	71	1964	L Piggott	140
1942	G Richards	67	1965	L Piggott	160
1943	G Richards	65	1966	L Piggott	191
1944	G Richards	88	1967	L Piggott	117
1945	G Richards	104	1968	L Piggott	139
1946	G Richards	212	1969	L Piggott	163
1947	G Richards	269	1970	L Piggott	162
1948	G Richards	224	1971	L Piggott	162
1949	G Richards	261	1972	W Carson	132
1950	G Richards	201	1973	W Carson	164
1951	G Richards	227	1974	P Eddery	148
1952	G Richards	231	1975	P Eddery	164
1953	G Richards	191	1976	P Eddery	162
1954	D Smith	129	1977	P Eddery	176
1955	D Smith	168	1978	W Carson	182
1956	D Smith	155	1979	J Mercer	164
1957	A Breasley	173	1980	W Carson	166
1958	D Smith	165	1981	L Piggott	179
1959	D Smith	157	1982	L Piggott	188
1960	L Piggott	170	1983	W Carson	159
1961	A Breasley	171			

LEADING OWNERS SINCE 1946

Year	Owner	Horses	Races Won	Value £
1946	HH Aga Khan	18	33	24,118
1947	HH Aga Khan	16	28	44,020
1948	HH Aga Khan	17	28	46,393
1949	HH Aga Khan	19	39	68,916
1950	M M Boussac	10	11	57,044
1951	M M Boussac	12	17	39,339
1952	HH Aga Khan	14	29	92,518
1953	Sir Victor Sassoon	23	39	58,579
1954	Her Majesty	10	19	40,993
1955	Lady Zia Wernher	2	6	46,345
1956	Maj LB Holliday	21	43	39,327
1957	Her Majesty	16	30	62,211
1958	Mr J McShain	2	6	63,264
1959	Prince Aly Khan	7	13	100,668
1960	Sir Victor Sassoon	15	29	90,069
1961	Maj LB Holliday	25	37	39,227
1962	Maj LB Holliday	24	39	70,206
1963	Mr JR Mullion	5	9	68,882

Year	Owner			Value £
1964	Mrs HE Jackson	2	3	98,270
1965	M J Ternynck	1	1	65,301
1966	Lady Zia Wernher	1	2	78,075
1967	Mr HJ Joel	22	34	120,925
1968	Mr Raymond R Guest	1	4	97,075
1969	Mr D Robinson	42	96	92,553
1970	Mr C Engelhard	20	30	182,059
1971	Mr P Mellon	11	22	138,786
1972	Mrs J Hislop	3	10	155,190
1973	Mr NB Hunt	7	11	124,771
1974	Mr NB Hunt	7	8	147,217
1975	Dr C Vittadini	6	12	209,492
1976	Mr D Wildenstein	5	10	244,500
1977	Mr R Sangster	16	21	348,023
1978	Mr R Sangster	15	27	160,405
1979	Sir M Sobell	5	13	339,751
1980	Mr S Weinstock	1	4	236,332
1981	HH Aga Khan	12	22	441,654
1982	Mr R Sangster	27	38	397,749
1983	Mr R Sangster	25	40	461,488

LEADING TRAINERS SINCE 1946

Year	Trainer	Value £	Year	Trainer	Value £
1946	Frank Butters	56,140	1963	PJ Prendergast (Ireland)	125,294
1947	F Darling	65,313	1964	PJ Prendergast (Ireland)	128,102
1948	CFN Murless	66,542	1965	PJ Prendergast (Ireland)	75,323
1949	Frank Butters	71,721	1966	MV O'Brien (Ireland)	123,848
1950	CH Semblat (France)	57,044	1967	CFN Murless	256,899
1951	JL Jarvis	56,397	1968	CFN Murless	141,508
1952	M Marsh	92,093	1969	AM Budgett	105,349
1953	JL Jarvis	71,546	1970	CFN Murless	199,524
1954	C Boyd-Rochfort	65,326	1971	I Balding	157,488
1955	C Boyd-Rochfort	74,424	1972	W Hern	206,767
1956	CF Elsey	61,621	1973	CFN Murless	132,984
1957	CFN Murless	116,898	1974	P Walwyn	206,445
1958	C Boyd-Rochfort	84,186	1975	P Walwyn	382,527
1959	CFN Murless	145,727	1976	H Cecil	261,301
1960	CFN Murless	118,327	1977	MV O'Brien (Ireland)	439,124
1961	CFN Murless	95,972	1978	H Cecil	382,812
1962	W Hern	70,206			

1979 H Cecil	683,971	1982 H Cecil	872,614
1980 W Hern	831,964	1983 W Hern	549,598
1981 M Stoute	723,786		

TOP STAKES WINNERS SINCE 1946

	Value £		Value £
1946 Airborne (3 yrs)	20,345	1965 Sea Bird II (3 yrs)	65,301
1947 Migoli (3 yrs)	17,215	1966 Charlottown (3 yrs)	78,075
1948 Black Tarquin (3 yrs)	21,423	1967 Royal Palace (3 yrs)	92,998
1949 Nimbus (3 yrs)	30,236	1968 Sir Ivor (3 yrs)	97,075
1950 Palestine (3 yrs)	21,583	1969 Blakeney (3 yrs)	63,108
1951 Supreme Court (3 yrs)	36,016	1970 Nijinsky (3 yrs)	159,681
1952 Tulyar (3 yrs)	75,173	1971 Mill Reef (3 yrs)	121,913
1953 Pinza (3 yrs)	44,101	1972 Brigadier Gerard (4 yrs)	151,213
1954 Never Say Die (3 yrs)	30,332	1973 Dahlia (3 yrs)	79,230
1955 Meld (3 yrs)	42,562	1974 Dahlia (4 yrs)	151,213
1956 Ribot (4 yrs)	23,727	1975 Grundy (3 yrs)	188,375
1957 Crepello (3 yrs)	32,257	1976 Wollow (3 yrs)	166,389
1958 Ballymoss (4 yrs)	38,686	1977 The Minstrel (3 yrs)	201,184
1959 Petite Etoile (3 yrs)	55,487	1978 Ile de Bourbon (3 yrs)	136,012
1960 St Paddy (3 yrs)	71,256	1979 Troy (3 yrs)	310,539
1961 Sweet Solera (3 yrs)	36,988	1980 Ela-Mana-Mou (3 yrs)	236,332
1962 Hethersett (3 yrs)	38,497	1981 Shergar (3 yrs)	295,654
1963 Ragusa (3 yrs)	66,011	1982 Kalaglow (4 yrs)	242,304
1964 Santa Claus (3 yrs)	72,067	1983 Sun Princess (3 yrs)	221,356

MULTIPLE CLASSIC WINNERS

The following is a list of the horses which have won two or more of the five Classic races.
(Key 2,000 Guineas 2G; 1,000 Guineas 1G; Derby D; Oaks O; St Leger L)

Winners of four Classics

Year	Horse	Classics
1868	Formosa	2G,1G,O,L
1902	Sceptre	2G,1G,O,L

Winners of three Classics

Year	Horse	Classics
1840	Crucifix	2G,1G,O
1853	West Australian	2G,D,L
1865	Gladiateur	2G,D,L
1866	Lord Lyon	2G,D,L
1871	Hannah	1G,O,L
1874	Apology	1G,O,L
1886	Ormonde	2G,D,L
1891	Common	2G,D,L
1892	La Fleche	1G,O,L
1893	Isinglass	2G,D,L
1897	Galtee More	2G,D,L
1899	Flying Fox	2G,D,L
1900	Diamond Jubilee	2G,D,L
1903	Rock Sand	2G,D,L
1904	Pretty Polly	1G,O,L
1915	Pommern	2G,D,L
1917	Gay Crusader	2G,D,L
1918	Gainsborough	2G,D,L
1935	Bahram	2G,D,L
1942	Sun Chariot	1G,O,L
1955	Meld	1G,O,L
1970	Nijinsky	2G,D,L

Winners of two Classics

Year	Horse	Classics
1800	Champion	D,L
1901	Eleanor	D,O
1813	Smolensko	2G,D
1817	Neva	1G,O
1818	Corinne	1G,O
1822	Pastille	2G,O
1823	Zinc	1G,O
1824	Cobweb	1G,O
1828	Cadland	2G,D
1832	Galata	1G,O
1835	Queen of Trumps	O,L
1836	Bay Middleton	2G,D
1843	Cotherstone	2G,D
1846	Sir Tatton Sykes	2G,L
	Mendicant	1G,O
1848	Surplice	D,L
1849	The Flying Dutchman	D,L
1850	Voltigeur	D,L
1852	Stockwell	2G,L
1857	Imperieuse	1G,L
	Blink Bonny	D,O
1858	Governess	1G,O
1862	The Marquis	2G,L
1863	Macaroni	2G,D
1864	Blair Athol	D,L
1867	Achievement	1G,L
1869	Pretender	2G,D
1872	Reine	1G,O
1873	Marie Stuart	O,L
1875	Spinaway	1G,O
1876	Petrarch	2G,L
	Camelia	1G,O
1877	Silvio	D,L
1878	Pilgrimage	2G,1G
	Jannette	O,L
1879	Wheel of Fortune	1G,O
1881	Thebais	1G,O
	Iroquois	D,L
1882	Shotover	2G,D
1884	Busybody	1G,O
1885	Melton	D,L
1886	Miss Jummy	1G,O
1887	Reve D'Or	1G,O
1888	Ayrshire	2G,D
	Seabreeze	O,L
1889	Donovan	D,L
1890	Memoire	O,L
1891	Mimi	1G,O
1894	Ladas	2G,D
	Amiable	1G,O
1895	Sir Visto	D,L
1896	Persimmon	D,L

Year	Horse	Code		Year	Horse	Code
1904	St Amant	2G,D		1940	Godiva	1G,O
1905	Cherry Lass	1G,O		1943	Herringbone	1G,L
1908	Signorinetta	D,O		1945	Sunstream	1G,O
1909	Minoru	2G,D		1946	Airborne	D,L
1911	Sunstar	2G,D		1947	Imprudence	1G,O
1912	Tagalie	1G,D		1949	Nimbus	2G,D
1913	Jest	1G,O			Musidora	1G,O
1914	Princess Dorrie	1G,O		1952	Tulyar	D,L
1916	Fifinella	D,O		1954	Never Say Die	D,L
1923	Tranquil	1G,L		1957	Crepello	2G,D
1925	Manna	2G,D		1958	Bella Paola	1G,O
	Saucy Sue	1G,O		1959	Petite Etoile	1G,O
1926	Coronach	D,L		1960	Never Too Late II	1G,O
1929	Trigo	D,L			St Paddy	D,L
1931	Cameronian	2G,D		1961	Sweet Solera	1G,O
1933	Hyperion	D,L		1967	Royal Palace	2G,D
1934	Windsor Lad	D,L		1968	Sir Ivor	2G,D
1937	Exhibitionnist	1G,O		1971	Altesse Royale	1G,O
1938	Rockfel	1G,O		1973	Mysterious	1G,O
1939	Blue Peter	2G,D		1977	Dunfermline	O,L
	Galatea	1G,O		1983	Sun Princess	O,L

Robert Sangster, leading owner.

OTHER RACING RECORDS

RIDING RECORDS IN THE CLASSICS

All Classics	Won
F Buckle (first Classic 1792)	27
L Piggott (1954)	26
J Robinson (1817)	24
F Archer (1874)	21

Most in each Classic		Won
2,000 Guineas	J Robinson	9
1,000 Guineas	G Fordham	7
Derby	L Piggott	9
Oaks	F Buckle	9
St Leger	W Scott	9

RIDING RECORDS

Gordon Richards, from 1921-54 rode 4,870 winners. In 1947 he won 269 races, in October 1933 he rode 12 consecutive winners, and was champion jockey 26 times—all records.

HORSES RECORDING MOST VICTORIES

Catherina, raced 1833-41, ran 176 times, won 79 races
Fisherman, raced 1855-9, ran 119 times, won 69 races
The Shadow, raced 1838-47, ran 114 times, won 64 races
Fisherman won 23 races in 1856

MOST SUCCESSFUL OWNER (RACES WON)

Miss Dorothy Paget, 1930-60, won 1,532 races
Mr David Robinson, 1973 - won 115 races

MOST SUCCESSFUL STALLION (RACES WON)

Stockwell (progeny raced between 1858-76) won 1,153 races - 132 in 1866

TRAINING RECORDS

Record prizemoney won in season	H Cecil (1982) £872,614
Most races won	H Cecil (1979) 128

FASTEST TIMES

Indigenous ran five furlongs at Epsom 2 June 1960 in 53.6 sec (41.97mph) hand timed.

Raffingora ran five furlongs at Epsom 5 June 1970 in 53.89 sec (41.75mph) electrical timing.

Mahmoud completed Derby course (1½ miles at Epsom) in 2 min 33.8 sec (35.06mph) 1936.

Miss Dorothy Paget leading in her Derby winner of 1943, Straight Deal.

THE RACECOURSES

Tony Stafford

ASCOT

Best known for its four-day June spectacular of high-class racing and eye-catching summer fashions, when it becomes Royal Ascot, this superb racecourse, situated in Berkshire less than 30 miles from Central London, always offers competitive sport. The track itself (right-handed) is very testing and over all distances, the ability to stay the trip is important. Much of the straight course, which extends for a mile, is uphill, so on soft ground, even sprints require plenty of stamina. On the round course, a circuit of which is a mile and threequarters, the last six furlongs are uphill, so long-distance races — Ascot stages events up to two and threequarter miles — are severe stamina tests. The short run-in, less than three furlongs, makes jockeyship a vital factor here.

Crowds in excess of 50,000 are common on Ascot Gold Cup day, but there are ample car parks to cope with the pressure, while Ascot Southern Region station (trains from Waterloo) is within walking distance.

The Ascot Gold Cup is one of 15 Group races run at the Royal meeting. On the first day (Tuesday) the Group races are the Queen Anne Stakes, Prince of Wales Stakes, St James's Palace Stakes, Coventry Stakes and Ribblesdale Stakes. The second day features the Jersey Stakes, Queen Mary Stakes, Coronation Stakes and Queen's Vase. Third day highlights, apart from the Gold Cup, are the Cork and Orrery Stakes, Norfolk Stakes and King Edward VII Stakes. On the last day, the Hardwicke Stakes and the sprint championship, the King's Stand Stakes, are pre-eminent. Also at the Royal meeting, the Royal Hunt Cup is one of the season's most important handicaps.

Other big races during the year are the King George VI and Queen Elizabeth Diamond Stakes — the most prestigious all-aged race run in England during the year (July) and in September the Hoover Fillies Mile, Diadem Stakes, Cumberland Lodge Stakes, Queen Elizabeth II Stakes (a top mile race) and the Royal Lodge Stakes, a mile two-year-old race contested by the following year's Classic candidates.

EFFECT OF DRAW: There is no significant advantage.

AYR

Situated on Scotland's south-west coast, Ayr is by far the most important of the country's three remaining racecourses — Edinburgh and Hamilton Park are the others. Ayr stages its important Western meeting in September, a four-day festival which has the Ladbroke Ayr Gold Cup, a six-furlong handicap, as the high point. Although no race at the meeting has Group status, the Doonside Cup, a conditions event over 11 furlongs, and the Harry Rosebery Challenge Trophy, for two-year-olds over five furlongs, always attract strong southern challenges.

The Ayr track, which is left-handed and oval, is about a mile
and a half in extent, and the run-in is half a mile. The going at
the September meeting is often soft, but generally the track
can be regarded as perfectly fair and a good test for the
strong, galloping type of horse.
  EFFECT OF DRAW: There is no significant advantage.

BATH

This popular West Country course, set in the hills a few miles
from the City centre, is a left-handed oval, of just over a mile
and a half, with a half-mile run-in. From the home turn, the
track bears slightly left all the way to the finish, and is uphill
throughout, putting a premium on stamina. In the past, a low
number draw near the rails was considered an advantage,
given the left-hand bias of the track, but more recent research
suggests that horses drawn high (towards the outside) find less
difficulty getting a run and thus may enjoy a slight advantage.
The five furlongs, five furlongs 167 yards, one mile and eight
yards, and two miles, one furlong and 27 yard races are
started on extensions to the track. The going in midsummer is
usually firm, but the old downland turf affords protection and
ensures that very soft going is rarely encountered.
  EFFECT OF DRAW: High numbers may have slight advantage
up to a mile.

BEVERLEY

Situated in south-east Yorkshire, close to Hull in Humberside,
Beverley is one racecourse where the draw is particularly
important. The five-furlong course on this right-hand circuit
joins the turn for home on the round course two and a half
furlongs out. High numbers, drawn on the far side, have the
benefit of the bend to the right just before the junction of the
courses, and with the track rising throughout the five furlongs,
stamina is vital. Two-year-old races early in the year, when
the going is often soft, are transformed frequently in the final
furlong. The round course, 11 furlongs in circumference,
contains a sharp downhill bend out of the back straight, but
the uphill finish gives the advantage in all races to the dour,
resolute galloper.
  EFFECT OF DRAW: High numbers best at five furlongs.

BRIGHTON

Britain's racecourses come in all shapes and sizes unlike those
in the United States which are mostly a mile round with a short
run-in. Brighton is one of the most unusual, following a course
along the top of a chalky-based hill with a valley between the
two portions which form the far and home straights. The
maximum distance at Brighton is a mile and a half. The course

first climbs, then falls and again rises before a sharp descent into the straight and then another final small rise. Thus Brighton is a track suitable for the sharp-actioned horse. The sprint course is also very sharp, with no separate straight, and here low numbers have an advantage in the draw as the track turns quite sharply left after a furlong. The course is situated a few miles along the Sussex coast from Brighton town centre, and draws many holidaymakers to its meetings, particularly in midsummer.

EFFECT OF DRAW: Low numbers favoured in sprints.

CARLISLE

If speed and adaptability are the key requirements for runners at Brighton, then exactly opposite characteristics are needed for the would-be Carlisle winner. Right-hand as against left, the track drains less well than its southern counterpart, and, particularly on soft going, the run from the home turn to the line is a real test of stamina. From four furlongs out, the track rises quite steeply before levelling off a furlong from home. Thus even sprints can be testing, with six-furlong races, always well contested, particularly finding out the non-stayer. The full circuit is just short of a mile and a half, and this distance is achieved by way of a shute, just after the winning post. The long-established Carlisle Bell, sponsored in 1983 by Tennant Caledonian, is run over a mile at the late June meeting. Local horses, from the Cumbrian region, do well here.

EFFECT OF DRAW: High numbers best up to a mile.

CATTERICK BRIDGE

Catterick, on the A1 in North Yorkshire, is better known as an army camp than the site of a racecourse, but this well-drained track is deservedly well-supported by trainers and racegoers alike. The course itself is just short of nine furlongs round, and left-handed. Its sharp turns and frequent undulations give a pronounced advantage to the quick-actioned, sharp type of horse. Sprints are invariably run — five furlongs from an extension to the straight, or six furlongs starting opposite the stands — at a tremendous gallop. The larger part of the track is downhill, and with two sharp bends to negotiate from six and seven furlongs races, a fast start is necessary to maintain the advantage given by a low draw near the rails.

EFFECT OF DRAW: Low numbers best up to seven furlongs.

CHEPSTOW

Chepstow, just the other side of the Severn Bridge in South Wales, is less important as a Flat racecourse than it is during the winter, when soft ground often makes its jumping course one of the most severe tests of a steeplechaser. The track is a

long, shallow oval, and extends (left-handed) for two miles.
The run-in is of five furlongs and the straight extends back to
give a straight mile. There are several changes of gradient,
with uphill, downhill and level portions which make the
straight a little awkward for the galloping type of stayer. In
midsummer the going is often extremely firm, which further
helps the sharper type of animal.

EFFECT OF DRAW: High numbers slightly favoured up to a
mile.

CHESTER

For three days each spring, the racecourse within the old
roman walls of the ancient city of Chester holds the interest of
the English racegoer. With its combination of classic trials,
helter-skelter sprints and the long-established Chester Cup,
racegoers have a well-balanced diet of first-class sport, all
perfectly visible to the naked eye on the smallest racecourse
in England. Chester is just a mile round. Called the 'Roodeye',
it is perfectly flat, always beautifully cultivated with the
greenest grass, it seems, anywhere in the country. Its
proximity to the River Dee, which runs around two-thirds of the
circuit makes flooding a problem in wet springs, and the
whole of the 1983 May meeting was lost for this reason. In
recent years Derby winners Henbit and Shergar warmed up for
the Epsom Derby by winning the Chester Vase, over the full
Classic distance of a mile and a half. Other important races at
the May meeting, in addition to the two and a quarter-mile
Chester Cup are the Ormonde Stakes, for top-class older
stayers, Cheshire Oaks, often a significant trial for possible
Epsom Oaks candidates, and the Dee Stakes. The small circuit
is on the turn almost throughout, thus in five and six furlong
races, a low draw near the rails is a big advantage. That
advantage can be totally nullified, though, by a slow start.
Strangely, horses apparently drawn worst of all on the wide
outside also win their share of races. This contradiction works
because whereas those in the middle of the field often find
difficulty in getting a clear run, those widest often get an
uninterrupted course.

EFFECT OF DRAW: Low numbers favoured up to seven and a
half furlongs.

DONCASTER

Each September, Yorkshire racing people puff out their chests
and flock to Doncaster for their own Classic, the St Leger. As
they proudly point out, the St Leger is the senior of the
Classics, having started on the Town Moor a few years before
its four southern counterparts. This long-distance event, run
over 14 furlongs and 127 yards has defied all attempts from its
detractors who would have its conditions altered to include

older horses as the Irish and French equivalents have. Specialisation in breeding makes the traditional 'Triple Crown' of 2,000 Guineas, Derby and St Leger, over a mile, mile and a half and 14½ furlongs respectively, almost impossible. Nijinsky, in 1970, was the last horse to achieve the feat, and is the only Triple Crown winner since the war. Other memorable winners were the Queen's Dunfermline in her Silver Jubilee year (1977), who beat the great Alleged, winner of the Arc de Triomphe for the next two years, and another great filly Sun Princess (1983).

Doncaster stages the first and last meetings of the flat season, with the William Hill Lincoln and William Hill November Handicap providing big betting races for spring and autumn. Other big races during the year are the Laurent Perrier Champagne Stakes, for two-year-olds, the Park Hill Stakes, the fillies' equivalent of the St Leger and the Doncaster Cup (2¼ miles). Doncaster is a flat galloping left-hand track 15 furlongs in circumference. The four and a half furlong run-in makes the track ideal for the galloping type of horse and the St Leger, usually truly run, is a formidable test of stamina.

EFFECT OF DRAW: Low numbers favoured in big fields up to a mile on straight course.

EDINBURGH

Scottish racegoers have to be content with three tracks. Ayr caters for the West Coast, and Hamilton Park serves Glasgow, while in the East Edinburgh's track is along the coast from the capital at Musselburgh. The track, which is right-hand, is situated close to the sands and is a narrow oval of ten furlongs with a half mile run-in. The two bends at the top end, out of the back straight and into the home straight are very sharp, making the course difficult for the galloping type of animal. Many races are won by a close railer at this point, and it is not uncommon for horses to win many times at the track by virtue of their adaptability.

EFFECT OF DRAW: High numbers best up to a mile.

EPSOM

When visitors from abroad first see Epsom racecourse, they are amazed that the world's best known Classic race could ever have been staged there. But both the Derby and the Oaks, apart from war-time transfer to Newmarket, have been retained at this downland track about 15 miles south of London, since the 18th century. A walk from the Derby start, a mile and a half from the finish, to the winning post, is even more astonishing, with regular changes in gradient and a number of difficult bends to negotiate. The stretch from the top of Tattenham Hill to Tattenham Corner a half-mile from the finish, is spectacular indeed, especially with a Derby field of

25 or so runners. Apart from the Derby, which is always run at a strong early gallop, most Epsom races require speed in excess of stamina, especially five furlongs. Epsom's five furlongs is the fastest in the world, the first furlong or so which is sharply downhill being the principal reason for this. The six and seven furlong starts are from shutes to the main track, and here, too, a fast start is necessary. Although the U-shaped track is only a mile and a half in extent, Epsom stages one long-distance race each year. The Great Metropolitan Handicap (2¼ miles) starts at the winning post, and after a run the reverse way along part of the straight, winds across the Downs in the middle of the track before rejoining the main track with just over a mile to race.

Apart from the Derby and the Oaks, Epsom is the home of Classic trials such as the Blue Riband Trial and Princess Elizabeth Stakes, while at the summer meeting, the Coronation Cup is an important target for the previous season's Classic colts and fillies.

EFFECT OF DRAW: Low numbers best up to eight and a half furlongs.

Epsom on Derby day 1971 as Mill Reef wins from Linden Tree.

FOLKESTONE

Situated at Westenhanger, a few miles inland from the Kent Channel port, Folkestone racecourse is a right-handed pear-shaped track of ten and a half furlongs. The six furlong straight is utilised for races of just over two miles. The track is undulating, but easy turns reduce the sharp overall nature. Neither is it truly galloping, despite the uphill finish. Folkestone rarely attracts top-class horses, although the Metropole Challenge Cup for two-year-olds has proved a magnet for some of the big stables. Kris, the mile champion of the late 1970's, began his career at this Kent course which has become more accessible with the development of the M20 motorway.

EFFECT OF DRAW: Low numbers slightly favoured in sprints.

GOODWOOD

Glorious Goodwood, a five-day summer racing spectacular in the most scenic setting in England, truly lives up to its name. From a vantage point on Trundle Hill, which dominates the scene after the winning post, the spectator can look across to get the best view of the action, most of which takes place a long way from the stands. Goodwood has no round course, but consists of a long loop, which enables the historic Goodwood Cup, over two miles and five furlongs to be staged. The horses start for the Cup at the winning post and take the longer of two routes back to the straight. The shorter route is reserved for one mile and seven furlong races, while the Stewards' Cup is the most famous race on the straight six furlongs. With several undulations, Goodwood is essentially sharp in nature, so speed is vital for all races except the Cup and other stayers events over two furlongs less. The summer meeting has a monopoly of the big races with the Sussex Stakes (one mile), Richmond Stakes (two-year-olds, six furlongs) and Gordon Stakes (three-year-olds, mile and a half) providing three historic highlights. The Waterford Crystal Mile and Waterford Candelabra Stakes (for two-year-old fillies) are highlights of the late August meeting.

EFFECT OF DRAW: High numbers slightly favoured in sprints.

HAMILTON PARK

Hamilton Park is to Glasgow what Musselburgh is to Edinburgh. Like its counterpart in the East, Hamilton offers modest fare, and like Edinburgh racecourse, has its share of regular winners. Unlike Edinburgh, Hamilton is not a complete circuit. The course consists of a six furlong straight with a right-handed loop. Races of 13 furlongs start at the winning post and return via the loop. The turns, again unlike Edinburgh are easy, while the finish is severe with a steep hill making stamina a necessity especially for two-year-olds early in the season, when the going tends to be soft.

EFFECT OF DRAW: Middle to high numbers best up to a mile.

HAYDOCK PARK

Haydock Park, with its first-class facilities, is one of the best racecourses in the country. Close to the M6 motorway at Newton-le-Willows in Lancashire, Haydock is easy to reach and the course itself is an excellent oval, 13 furlongs in circumference. The run-in of four and a half furlongs, slightly uphill throuhout, tests the stamina of a racehorse and makes Haydock a galloping circuit. This is even more noticeable during wet weather when the best going is often to be found under the stands rails, changing the effect of the draw in such conditions. Haydock stages the Lancashire Oaks and Old Newton Cup, a long established handicap, during the summer, while the highlight of Haydock's autumn programme is the Vernon's Sprint Cup, one of the most important tests for sprinters during the season.

EFFECT OF DRAW: Low numbers slightly favoured on round course. On soft ground high numbers best at five and six furlongs.

KEMPTON PARK

With the passing of Alexandra Park, London no longer boasts its own racecourse. Kempton Park, at Sunbury-on-Thames is nearest to the centre of the capital, and is next to the London end of the M3 motorway. The track itself is a 13-furlong right-handed triangle, with a three and a half furlong run-in. There is a separate 'Jubilee' course, ten furlongs in extent which joins the round course at the turn for home. Sprint races are run on another separate diagonal course. The six furlong start is close to the seven furlong Jubilee start and crosses the round course. The straight course has its own winning post further from the stands and close finishes are often difficult to interpret. Kempton is flat, except for the first two furlongs on the Jubilee, which are slightly downhill, and is neither sharp nor galloping in character. Kempton is the home of several long-established and famous handicaps, notably the Queen's Prize, Rosebery Stakes and Jubilee Stakes, while the September Stakes has become an important race for high-class middle-distance horses.

EFFECT OF DRAW: Low numbers slightly favoured up to a mile.

LEICESTER

Leicester racecourse is a true test of stamina. The mile and threequarter circuit is not used in its entirety for Flat racing, the longest race being a mile and a half, beginning at the end of the back straight and joining the straight mile about four and a half furlongs from home. Soon after, the track rises for two furlongs before levelling off two furlongs from the finish. On the straight course the first half mile is slightly downhill. Bends on the round course are easy and well-cambered and, especially at the beginning of the season on softish going, two-year-olds find the five furlongs quite severe.

EFFECT OF DRAW: No significant advantage.

LINGFIELD PARK

Lingfield Park has many of the characteristics of Epsom's Derby
course, so it is an ideal track on which to test Derby and Oaks
candidates' ability to handle Epsom. The Derby and Oaks Trials
in May offer significant pointers to Classic hopes each year.
The round course contains a similar rise to that of Epsom, while
the downhill run to a sharp turn into the straight is almost a
replica of the run down to Tattenham Corner. The straight
course at Lingfield is almost a mile, and is steeply downhill
until the straight is reached, from which point the gradient is
less marked, until two furlongs from the finish when it levels
out to the winning post. Speed and adaptability are the
principal requirements for Lingfield, a track on which the
dour, galloping type is at a distinct disadvantage.

   EFFECT OF DRAW: High numbers slightly favoured up to
seven furlongs and 140 yards.

NEWBURY

Newbury racecourse, close to the Berkshire town's centre and
within easy reach of the M4 motorway is one of the fairest
tracks in the country. It is a left-hand oval of about 15 furlongs,
with both a straight mile and a round mile, the latter starting
on an extension to the round course proper. Although there
are slight undulations, Newbury is galloping in nature and a
five furlong run-in provides a good stamina test. Important
races include the Greenham Stakes and Fred Darling Stakes
(Guineas trials for colts and fillies respectively), in April, the
Lockinge Stakes for milers in May, the Hungerford Stakes
(seven furlongs) and Geoffrey Freer (13 furlongs) in August,
the Mill Reef Stakes (two-year-olds) in September and Horris
Hill Stakes (seven furlongs) and St Simon Stakes (mile and a
half) in October.

   EFFECT OF DRAW: High numbers slightly favoured on
straight course.

NEWCASTLE

The 14-furlong Newcastle racecourse at High Gosforth Park
just outside the town is one of the toughest tests of stamina in
the country. The last five furlongs and less are run on the
straight course, and two-year-olds often find this track
extremely testing, particularly at the beginning of the season
when the going is often soft or heavy. The bends are easy, so
the course is galloping in nature. The most important race of
the year at Newcastle is the Northumberland Plate, known as
the Pitmen's Derby, run in late June over two miles. At the
same meeting, the Gosforth Park Cup, over five furlongs,
attracts top-class sprint handicappers.

   EFFECT OF DRAW: No advantage.

NEWMARKET

Newmarket is the headquarters of horse racing, and since Stuart times racing has been conducted on an organised basis on this vast expanse of Heathland on the borders of Cambridgeshire and Suffolk. Commentators always preface their remarks — accurately — about the Cesarewitch, the second leg of the Autumn Double — the Cambridgeshire is the first — by saying that the race starts in Cambridgeshire and finishes in Suffolk. The scale of Newmarket is such that two distinct racecourses have been established. The better-known Rowley Mile is used in spring and autumn, while the July course is reserved for summer racing. The first part of each is common. Races up to two miles on the July course and two and a quarter miles on the Rowley Mile separate at the junction of the courses, one mile from the July finish and 11 furlongs from the end of the Rowley Mile. The July course has a sharper right-hand bend into the mile straight. The two courses have contrasting stands, those on the Rowley Mile being modern and functional with much greater spectator capacity than those of the more rustic, relaxed July course.

Rowley Mile

All races up to 10 furlongs are run on a straight course. There was a round course previously , but this proved unpopular with trainers as it was not watered and provided firmer ground than was customary on the straight and July courses. The course is wide, drains well and provides a fair test for a racehorse. It is galloping in nature and the uphill finish is very testing. Big races run on the Rowley Mile include the two spring Classics, the 2,000 Guineas and 1,000 Guineas; the Champion Stakes, Cambridgeshire and Cesarewitch in the autumn. Other big races include the Craven Stakes, Nell Gwyn Stakes and Free Handicap (April), Jockey Club Stakes (Guineas meeting), Jockey Club Cup and Sun Chariot Stakes. Two-year-olds contest important juvenile championship tests in the Middle Park, Cheveley Park and Dewhurst Stakes.
  EFFECT OF DRAW: No advantage.

July Course

Summer racing at Newmarket is much more informal than during the big meetings of spring and autumn. The July Course invariably provides excellent going even in the driest summer and fields are always competitive. The highlight is the three-day July meeting which features the July Cup, one of the year's top sprints, the July Stakes, for two-year-olds and the Bunbury Cup, a top-class seven-furlong handicap. Like its counterpart course across the county border, the July Course suits the resolute galloper.
  EFFECT OF DRAW: No advantage.

NOTTINGHAM

Nottingham racecourse, situated just north of the town in Colwick Park, is a fair, flat mile and a half circuit. The left hand track has a four and a half furlong run-in and easy turns while the straight course stages all races over five and six furlongs. Nottingham attracts good handicappers for the sprint races, notably the Nottingham Stewards Cup, which often gives Goodwood failures a chance to make amends.

EFFECT OF DRAW: High numbers favoured up to six furlongs.

PONTEFRACT

The left-hand Pontefract track, two miles in extent, has recently been modified to accommodate races up to two and a half miles. Previously the longest distance used was a mile and a half, but the circuit was completed in 1982 to allow for these long-distance races. Pontefract has severe undulations and in races of six furlongs, runners encounter first a descent, then a rise, then another fall before a sharp uphill gradient all the way to the finish. The home turn is only two furlongs out, so while stamina is essential for longer races, sprints are less suitable for galloping types by dint of the changes in gradient and the bend after halfway. Generally racing is fairly low key, although the management has been very go-ahead in improving facilities and attracting better-class runners with their Mile Championship series for three-year-olds. A low draw is a big help in sprints, although a slow start nullifies it.

EFFECT OF DRAW: Low numbers best.

REDCAR

In the early days of sponsorship, Redcar was a flourishing holiday racetrack in the north-east, but finances were rather strained by the end of the 1970's. Since then a lively management have effected a recovery for this intimate Yorkshire course. The track is a very narrow oval, about 14 furlongs round, with a straight run-in of five furlongs. Races up to a mile are straight and the course, which is flat throughout offers a good gallop for the long-striding type of animal. While some sponsors no longer support Redcar, the William Hill Gold Cup and Andy Capp Handicap remain, and still attract good fields.

EFFECT OF DRAW: No advantage.

RIPON

The right-handed Ripon circuit extends for 13 furlongs. The run-in of five furlongs joins the six furlong straight course. Throughout the straight, the ground rises and falls. These undulations and sharp, cramped bends have the effect of making the course unsuitable for the galloping type of horse. The straight gives little draw advantage, but mile races, which start towards the end of the back straight, favour high numbers which get the help of an inside run round the two bends. Major races at Ripon include the Ripon Two-year-old Trophy, the Ripon Rowels Handicap and the six-furlong Great St Wilfrid Handicap.

EFFECT OF DRAW: High numbers best at one mile.

SALISBURY

Salisbury racecourse consists of a straight mile and a narrow loop which enables races of up to a mile and threequarters to be run. For this distance, the horses race away from the stands, around the loop and rejoin the straight course six furlongs from home. From here the course is uphill all the way to the finish, so all races are a test of stamina, particularly when the going is soft, as it often is at the spring meeting where Classic trials for colts and fillies are run. Under these conditions, the ground usually favours horses drawn in the low numbers, although generally the draw has little significance.

EFFECT OF DRAW: No significant advantage, although low numbers favoured on soft ground in sprints.

SANDOWN PARK

This popular racecourse, within easy reach of London on the M3 is situated at the end of Esher High Street in Surrey, and set in a perfect amphitheatre which makes it the best natural viewing arena of any English racecourse. The track, which is right-hand, is 13 furlongs round and throughout the four-furlong run-in, there is a steady rise to the finish. Five furlong races are run on a separate course through the middle of the main oval, and this too is uphill all the way. Stamina and the ability to gallop are therefore of paramount importance and since the modification of what was formerly a difficult bend on the far turn, the long-striding type of horse is even better suited.

The most important race of the year at Sandown is the Coral-Eclipse Stakes over ten furlongs, which gives Classic three-year-olds a chance to be tested against the best older horses. In April the Guardian Classic Trial has unearthed several Derby winners and shares a brilliant Whitbread Gold Cup day programme with the Westbury Stakes. That ten furlong race attracts similar horses to the Brigadier Gerard Stakes a month later when the Temple Stakes (sprint) and Henry II Stakes (two-miles) are the other features. The round course seems to offer little advantage to high or low-drawn horses, but in five furlong races on soft ground, horses drawn high in big fields have a singificant advantage.

EFFECT OF DRAW: High numbers best at five furlongs on soft ground in big fields.

THIRSK

The left-handed Thirsk track is ten furlongs in extent, and with its undulating run-in of about half a mile, is against the galloping type of horse. There is a six-furlong straight track which is undulating throughout. Horses drawn on the outside in the low numbers have a disadvantage.

EFFECT OF DRAW: High numbers best up to six furlongs.

WARWICK

Although the Warwick circuit is more than a mile and threequarters round, it cannot be considered ideal for a galloping type of horse because of the sharp bend into the straight and the short run-in of about three and a half furlongs. There is no straight sprint course, and five-furlong races start on a shute to the main track. A fast start at this distance is essential and a low draw under such circumstances helps greatly as they negotiate the bend into the straight approaching halfway. Races beyond a mile are less difficult for the galloping type of horse, but up to a mile the sharp, quick-actioned type is ideal.

EFFECT OF DRAW: Low numbers best in sprints.

WINDSOR

Uniquely among British Flat racecourses, Windsor is laid out as a figure of eight with two loops joining at the intersection about three furlongs from the finish. The course, by the side of the River Thames is a mile and a half in extent and turns both left and right. Handiness is thus essential, although the sharp nature of the track is lessened somewhat by the five furlong run-in. There is a six-furlong straight course, which like the rest of the circuit is level throughout. Windsor specialises in three-year-old races and often high-class horses begin their careers here. Most meetings during the summer are run during the evenings and attendances are usually large, as are fields, particularly when the going is good.

EFFECT OF DRAW: High numbers favoured in sprints.

WOLVERHAMPTON

The left handed Wolverhampton track is triangular in shape and a mile and a half in extent. There is a straight five furlongs and the track, level throughout, favours neither the galloping nor the sharp-actioned type of horse.

EFFECT OF DRAW: No advantage.

YARMOUTH

Yarmouth racecourse is a popular summer attraction for holidaymakers at this Norfolk resort. Meetings are held regularly through the holiday months, and often stars of the future make their debuts as two-year-olds, Newmarket trainers especially finding this a suitable testing ground. The track, 13 furlongs round, has a five furlong run-in. There is a straight mile and the course, close to the sea, is perfectly flat and thus not difficult for an inexperienced two-year-old to cope with.

EFFECT OF DRAW: No advantage.

YORK

York racecourse is situated on the Knavesmire, close to the City Centre and is one of the principal racecourses in the country. Set out as a wide U-shape, York is two miles in extent, with a six-furlong straight course and just two sweeping bends. York is perfectly flat and the five furlong run-in ensures that the galloping type of horse has every chance. Seven furlong races are started at a spur to the main track. York has a spring and a summer festival as well as a big charity day in early summer. At the May meeting, Classic trials such as the Mecca-Dante and Musidora Stakes and the Yorkshire Cup are the important races. In summer, the highlight is the Tote-Ebor, one of the best-known and most fiercely contested handicaps of the year, while the Benson and Hedges Gold Cup, William Hill Sprint, Gimcrack Stakes and Yorkshire Oaks are all races attracting top-class horses. The June charity day, organised by Timeform, has raised considerable sums for Cancer Research.

EFFECT OF DRAW: Low numbers have slight advantage up to six furlongs especially on soft going.

Pat Eddery, three times winner of the Benson and Hedges Gold Cup run at York.

READING FORM

Adrian Hunt

Reading form — studying horses' previous performances in order to assess their future prospects — is all a matter of interpretation. Everybody who makes the effort to study form closely has access to the same information but as in most things, opinion differs as to what represents good, bad or indifferent form.

Every daily newspaper provides a list of runners for each race meeting taking place on the day they publish and most provide form figures for each runner.

Form figures indicate where a certain horse has finished on each of its last six outings; 1 = 1st, 2 = 2nd, 0 = not in first 4. But these figure alone only tell what happened to the horse last time out and not far more important considerations like who it beat, who beat it, and by how far. Some papers, including *The Daily Telegraph*, provide an abbreviated version of a horse's actual form last time out, in addition to its last six place figures.

Enthusiasts wishing to make a more detailed study of horse racing form should buy either the all-racing newspaper *The Sporting Life* or subscribe to the Form Book, in addition to their normal daily newspaper. The Form Book, which is the official record of horseracing results in Britain, is called 'Raceform Up-to-Date'. It is a loose-leaf book which builds into a full volume as the season progresses and comes in weekly instalments which can be ordered from a newsagent or obtained direct from Raceform, 2 York Road, Battersea, London SW11.

As well as giving the finishing position of each horse that contested a past race, the Form Book also tells you how the horse looked in the parade ring beforehand and gives a detailed description of how it ran. Listed below are the abbreviations used by the Form Book for both Flat and National Hunt racing and accepted throughout the racing world.

HOW THEY LOOKED IN THE PADDOCK

v nice c = very nice colt: outstanding on looks
nice c = nice colt: very good sort
gd sort = well made: above average on looks
wl grwn = well grown: furnished to frame
w'like = workmanlike
h.d.w. = has done well: improved in looks
scope = scope for development
cmpt = compact

lt-f = light-framed
unf = unfurnished: not furnished to frame
nt grwn = not grown
lw = looked well
bkwd = backward in condition
str = strong
swtg = sweating excessively
t = tubed
b = bandaged fore leg
b.hind = bandaged hind leg
H = hood or blinkers

btn = beaten
bttr = better
c = came
cd = could
ch = chance
chal = challenge(d)
chsd = chased
circ = circuit
cl = close
cld = claimed
clr = clear
comf = comfortable
crse = course
ct = caught
dismntd = dismounted
dist = distance
(240 yds from winning post)
disq = disqualified
div = division
drvn = driven
dspt = dispute(d)
dwlt = dwelt
early = early
edgd = edged
effrt = effort
ent = entering
ev ch = every chance
extra = extra
f = furlong
fdd = faded
fin = finished
fnc = fence
fnd = found
fnl = final
fr = from
gd = good
gng = going
grad = gradually
grnd = ground
½ way = half way
hd = head
hdd = headed
hdl = hurdle
hdwy = headway
hl = hill
hld = held
hmpd = hampered
hrd rdn = hard ridden

imp = impression
impd = improved
ins = inside
j.b = jumped badly
jnd = joined
jst = just
j.w = jumped well
kpt = kept
l = length
lckd = lacked
ld = lead
ldr = leader
lft = left
lkd = looked
ltl = little
m = mile
mde = made
mde virt all = made virtually all
m.n.s = made no show
mid div = middle division
mstke(s) = mistake(s)
n.d = no danger
n.g.t = not go through
nk = neck
n.m.r = not much room
no ex = no extra pace
no imp = no impression
nr = near
nrr = nearer
nrst fin = nearest at finish
nt = not
nvr = never
nxt = next
o.d = open ditch
one pce = one paced
out = from finish
outpcd = outpaced
pce = pace
pckd = pecked
pl = place
plcd = placed
plld = pulled
press = pressure
prog = progress
prom = prominent
p.u. = pulled up
qckn = quicken
quickly = quickly

r = race
racd = raced
rch = reach
reard = reared
rcvr = recover
rdn = ridden
ref = refused
rm = room
rntd = remounted
rn = ran
rng = running
r.o = ran on
rr = rear
rn wl = ran well
rspnse = response
rt = right
s = start
sddle = saddle
s.h = short head
shkn = shaken
shld = should
shwd = showed
s.i.s = slowly into stride
slt = slight
sme = some
sn = soon
spd = speed
sqzd = squeezed
s.s = started slowly
st = straight
stdy = steady
stdd = steadied
str = strong

strtnd = straightened
styd = stayed
s.u. = slipped up
swtchd = switched
swvd = swerved
tch = touch
th = there
than = than
thro = through
thrght = throughout
tk = took
tl = until
t.n.p = took no part
t.o = tailed off
trbld = troubled
unable = unable
uns = unseated
u.p = under pressure
uphl = uphill
v = very
virt = virtually
w = with
wd = wide
whn = when
wknd = weakened
wl = well
wnr = winner
wnt = went
w.r.s = whipped round start
wt = weight
wtr = water
wy = way

Once you have familiarised yourself with these symbols, you are ready to start reading form.

The Form Book lists each race of the season under an index number for easy reference. There is an alphabetical list of all the horses which have run during the season at the back of the book. The index numbers of all the races they have contested appear on the right of each name.

Opposite is a race taken from the 1983 Flat season Form Book, with an explanation of what the various symbols mean.

It took place on Saturday 27 August and the official going (state of the ground) was considered to be good to firm. The index number of the race was 2303 and it was called the Blackgate Handicap. Horses are rated from 0-100 for handicapping purposes and the handicap range for this race

2031—NEWCASTLE (L-H)
Saturday, August 27th [Good to firm]   Wind: slight half against   Vis:moderate after 3rd
Going Allowance: 0.05 sec per fur (G)

Stalls: high   BLACKGATE H'CAP (0-35) £1990.40 (£554.40: £267.20)   **1m 2f**   1-45 (1-46)

2303

21324 **Mystic Margaret** (AGHide) 4—8-2‡[7] KWilliams (9) (lw: bhd: gd hdwy 2f out: rdn to ld wl ins fnl f) .... —1
2054* San Fermin (Fav) (JGFitzGerald) 4—8-4 MWood (7) (lw: 5th st: slt ld dist: nt qckn nr fin) nk.2
2132* Comtec Princess (MJRyan) 4—8-11 (8x) ‡[7] AWeiss (15) (3rd st: ev ch dist: kpt on wl u.p) nk.3
21144 Roger Nicholas (HWharton) 4—7-12‡[7] MFozzard (3) (lw: hdwy on ins 2f out; r.o) ¾.4
2042 Scoutsmistake (BAMcMahon) 4—8-9 AMackay (4) (hdwy over 2f out: ev ch over 1f out: onepcd) ½.5
918 Jacinto Times (USA) (MrsMNesbitt) 4—8-7 ACrook (8) (styd on fnl 3f: nvr able chal) 3.6
18953 Sallametti (USA) (WBentley) 5—7-11 EJohnson (11) (led over 7f: sn btn) 7
2208 Sheba's Glory (FWatson) 5—8-9‡[3] MFry (14) (2nd st: led over 2f out tl wknd qckly dist) 8
2197 Heckley Hinny (GBBalding) 3—9-0 JBleasdale (10) (nvr nr ldrs) 9
1320 Oration (CWThornton) 4—9-7‡[3] ANesbitt (12) (4th st: wknd over 3f out: 14) 0
16414 Banoco (TCraig) 5—9-9 NConnorton (13) (swtg: nvr nr ldrs: 11) 0
19153 Kitty Frisk (JWWatts) 3—8-5 EHide (2) (prom: rdn appr st: sn btn: 13) 0
2183 Manx Swallow (RHollinshead) 4—7-9‡[5] WRyan (6) (n.d: 10) 0
1922 Track Sharp (MrsMNesbitt) 4—7-13 JLowe (16) (lw: dwlt: a bhd: 16) 0
1517 The Aspel (bl) (DWChapman) 5—7-4‡[5] SHorsfall (5) (prom tl wknd qckly & 6th st: 12) 0
1846 Delirah (CWCElsey) 3—7-8 LCharnock (1) (bhd & rdn appr st: n.d: 15) 0

11/4 San Fermin, **13/2** Comtec Princess, **7/1** Scoutsmistake, **10/1** Roger Nicholas, Sallametti (USA)(tchd 20/1), **11/1** Kitty Frisk, **12/1** Heckley Hinny, **14/1** MYSTIC MARGARET, Banoco, **20/1** Oration, Delirah, **33/1** Ors. CSF £48.31, CT £251.13. Tote £13.00:£2.00 £1.10 £2.00 £4.20 (£15.30). Mr Wm Bates (NEWMARKET) bred by Patricia Ryan, 16 Rn.

2m 10.09 (4.09)
SF—52/53/59/44/54/46

was (0-35) which means that it was an event for moderate horses only. The winner's prize was £1,990.40, the second received £554.40 and the third horse £267.20. The race was run over one and a quarter miles.

Mystic Margaret's previous outing was in race number 2132 of the Form Book and she had finished fourth. She is trained by AG Hide, and is four years old. She carried 8 st and 2 lbs — this included the weight of her rider, the rest being made up by lead in her saddle-cloth.

But she had been originally set to carry 8 st 9 lb, the 7lb reduction being the riding allowance of her apprentice jockey, K Williams. Apprentices and amateur riders are allowed claims (weight concessions) when they are competing against fully-fledged jockeys. Depending on their length of experience and the number of winners they have ridden, this allowance varies from 7 lb to 3 lb. Most apprentices and amateurs truly need this concession when riding against the professionals and so in this case for instance, it is wiser to ignore K Williams's 7 lb claim and regard Mystic Margaret as having carried her full 8 st 9 lb.

Mystic Margaret was drawn in stall 9. The draw would have

been of little significance in a race over this distance but a high or low number in the draw can be of great importance at some courses, particularly over sprint distances of five, six or seven furlongs. The effect of the draw for each course is listed in the front of the Form Book and is also published in every daily newspaper when applicable.

The horse looked well in the paddock beforehand — in other words, she looked fit enough to produce her best form. She was behind in the early stages of the race but made good headway two furlongs from home and was ridden to lead well inside the final furlong. She started at 14-1 in pre-race betting and won by a neck from San Fermin who started favourite at 11-4.

San Fermin had previously run in race 2054, which he won. He also looked well in the paddock; he was in fifth place entering the home straight, held a slight lead at the distance — 240 yards from the winning post — but was unable to find the necessary speed near the finish.

Comtec Princess, second favourite at 13-2, finished a further neck behind the first two horses in third place. She, like San Fermin, had won her previous race. But her win had come in a later race than his and the handicapper did not have time to reassess her merit as far as this race was concerned.

The handicapper has a safety net called a penalty in cases like this. A penalty is a fixed amount of extra weight a horse has to carry if it wins — and therefore shows improved form — after the weights for the race in question have been published.

Comtec Princess was originally set to carry 8 st 10 lb in the Blackgate Handicap but she incurred an 8 lb penalty which brought her weight up to 9 st 4 lb. She did not carry 9 st 4 lb in the event though because the 7 lb claim of her rider, A Weiss, brought her weight down to 8 st 11 lb. As in Mystic Margaret's case, it is best to regard her as having carried her full weight of 9 st 4 lb from a form-study point of view.

Weight is translated into terms of distance in horseracing but the translation varies according to the distance over which a race is run. Form students have varying ideas about this translation but the following table is used by *The Daily Telegraph* and while not as complicated as some, it has stood the test of time.

RACES OVER 5 furlongs, 6f and 7f
short head, head and neck   = 1 lb
½-length   = 1½ lb
1-length   = 3 lb

RACES OVER 1 mile to 1½ miles
short head, head, neck and ½-length = 1 lb
1-length   = 2 lb

RACES OVER 1 mile and upwards and all National Hunt races
1-length   = 1 lb

It can be concluded that Mystic Margaret would not have won the race in question—and would probably have finished out of the first two—had she carried an additional 2 lb.

The penalties which horses incur for winning a race are *fixed* amounts of weight and they do not take into account how easily a horse managed to win. Using the above weight and distance table, we can estimate that Mystic Margaret had only 1 lb in hand when winning at Newcastle. She carried a 5 lb penalty for that success in a subsequent race at Chepstow and, as can be seen below, the extra 4 lb in the penalty probably made the difference between victory and defeat the next time out.

```
2531   BRECON H'CAP (0-35) £1281.60 (£357.60: £172.80)  1m 2f       3-30 (3-32)
                        (Weights raised 3 lb)
2448 Tower Win (CJBenstead) 6–7–8‡3 RHills (8) (lw: 5th st: led over 3f out: rdn fnl f.
            r.o) ............................................................................ —1
2303* Mystic Margaret (Jt-Fav) (AGHide) 4–8-6 (5x) ‡7 KWilliams (6) (8th st: hdwy 3f
            out: ev ch 1f out: unable qckn) .................................. 1½.2
1392 Relda (RJBaker) 3–8-6(3) CAsmussen (10) (lw: hld up: gd hdwy fnl 2f: nrst fin) .... 1½.3
2302* Floyd (MMadgwick) 3–9-0 (5x) IJohnson (9) (7th st: styd on: nvr nr to chal) ...... 2½.4
2335³ Sir Humphrey (bl) (Jt-Fav) (BSwift) 3–8-9 RFox (3) (4th st: rdn over 2f out: one
            pce fnl f) ...................................................... 1½.5
2190 Afzal (MRStoute) 3–9-2 AKimberley (7) (bhd: stdy hdwy fnl 2f: nt rch ldrs) ........ 1½.6
2144 Leonidas (USA) (DWPArbuthnot) 5–9-10 PCook (2) (led 1f: 6th st: effrt u.p 3f
            out: no imp) .................................................... 3.7
2428 Belle Vue (RHollinshead) 10–7-11(9)‡7 CNolan (4) (a in rr) ........................ 3.8
      Fit for a King (JWebber) 4–8-2(2)‡7 SKeightley (1) (led after 1f tl 3f out: sn btn) ... 9
2357 Last Gunboat (APIngham) 3–8-1 RCurant (11) (3rd st: wknd 3f out: 10) ............. 0
2042 Bright Spirit (RJBaker) 3–7-7 RStreet (5) (w ldrs: 2nd st: wknd over 2f out: 11) ... 0
7/2 Mystic Margaret, Sir Humphrey, 5/1 Afzal, 7/1 Floyd, 8/1 TOWER WIN, 9/1 Leonidas (USA), 10/1 Relda,
16/1 Bright Spirit, 25/1 Fit for a King, 33/1 Ors. CSF £34.24, CT £258.64  Tote £10.50: £1.90 £1.70 £2.30
(£11.80). Mr D. Turner (EPSOM) bred by Collinstown Stud Farm Ltd, 11 Rn.         2m 10.1 (4.1)
                                                                        SF –9/18/15/18.10/14
```

Relda, who finished third in the race, carried 8 st 6 lb as can be seen. But Relda had been handicapped with only 8 st 3 lb originally and had to carry the additional 3 lb because his jockey, C Asmussen, weighed that much heavier than 8 st 3 lb.

This extra 3 lb is termed as '3 lb overweight'. Thankfully for the form student, jockeys putting up overweight is not a common occurrence. An even more glaring example of it in this race was Belle Vue who finished eighth.

Belle Vue was set to carry 7 st 9 lb and C Nolan's 7 lb claim should have brought the weight down to 7 st 2 lb. But C Nolan weighs 7 st 11 lb and Belle Vue was therefore forced to carry overweight of 9 lb.

Weights of all the riders are published at the back of the Form Book and it is always worth checking that any horse you may fancy does not have to carry needless overweight which will obviously have a detrimental effect on its prospects. *The Sporting Life*, published daily, uses the same information as the Form Book, but they employ their own team of racereaders to provide remarks for each runner and present the form in a different fashion. Mystic Margaret's 27 August Newcastle form would appear in *The Sporting Life* on the day she contested the subsequent race at Chepstow. Belle Vue would be shown in Mystic Margaret's line of form at Nottingham on 9 August because he was running against her again at Chepstow.

The official going for each meeting is published in every daily newspaper. Certain horses have a distinct liking for either firm or soft ground and are unable to produce their best form on the opposite type of going.

Time also plays a part when assessing form. But many middle and long distance races are run at a false pace and time has more significance in five and six furlong sprints which tend to be run at a true pace.

The race we are considering at Newcastle was run in 2 min 10.9 sec. The figure in brackets (4.09) after the time represents the number of seconds slower than "standard time", in which the race was run. Standard time is the average over the 10 best recent times run over the course and distance, corrected to allow for variations of weight and state of going. A minus sign would indicate a time faster than standard. Sometimes "a" is used for "above", or slower, than standard, "b" for "below" average.

But weight and distances between the horses in a race provide the base of form study and a strict interpretation of these two factors is of paramount importance.

Studying form is a time-consuming business however and those who haven't the patience for the task but still require a sound form guide would do well to subscribe to Timeform.

'Timeform', published weekly by Portway Press Ltd, Halifax, West Yorkshire, HX1 1XE, is a large black-covered volume which provides an updated rating for every horse that has appeared.

In addition to a rating, 'Timeform' also gives comment on the horse's background, its characteristics, which type of going it prefers and how far it can be expected to stay.

Daniel Coupland

THE BETTING SYSTEM

Britain is practically the only country where bookmakers are both legal and dominate the racing scene, with their 11250 betting shops attracting an off-course turnover of £3,075 million in 1982-83.

Betting Offices were first legalised under the Betting and Gaming Act of 1960 and the £20,079,101 they paid to the Horserace Betting Levy Board in 1982-83 goes towards funding the industry.

Before the Act came into force, bets could only be made at the racecourse, through a credit account or via a runner who would collect the illegal bets from the corner of a street and pass them on to a bookmaker. But once the clause legalising betting shops came into force on the 1st May 1961, the simple task of writing the name of the horse and size of the bet on a slip of paper proved fruitful for the bookmakers and the number of offices soon mushroomed.

The street runner then became almost obsolete until the introduction of a 2½ per cent betting tax in 1966, but the number of illegal bets has grown along with the upward trend in tax which went to 5 per cent in 1969, to 6 per cent in 1970, 7½ per cent in 1974 and 8 per cent in 1981. Last year there were an estimated £500 million in illegal bets.

Some £246 million was paid to the government in off-course betting tax for 1982-3, but much more could have been collected had some bookmakers not been driven underground by the ever increasing spiral of taxation.

Although the government charged only 8 per cent of each off-course bet made, in most betting offices a further 2 per cent is added making a 10 per cent deduction in all. The extra per cent helps cover a levy which is paid to the Horserace Betting Levy Board and Value Added Tax which by law cannot be claimed by bookmakers. Racecourse bets are taxed at 4 per cent and no extra costs are incurred.

HISTORY OF BETTING

As early as 3200 BC betting on horses was recorded when two lesser nobles of two rival Arab sheiks matched their selected horses in a 12-mile race for a stake of 100 camels. When the two best horses began to draw away from the rest, the onlookers surged onto the course and began hurling missiles at the other horses to speed them up. This led to a war that lasted a century with the two tribes virtually destroying themselves.

Big bets would create a stir today but more than 100 years ago noblemen like Lord George Bentinck would often bet hundreds of thousands on the Derby which is Britain's biggest betting race with an estimated £20 million turnover in 1983.

In the 1946 Derby an American millionaire used the $6,000 he had made on a stock-exchange deal to back a horse called Airborne. He backed the horse at 50-1 and although Airborne won at much shorter odds the millionaire went home $3,000,000 richer.

The Grand National is second only to the Derby as a betting medium and from the bookmakers' point of view one of the most remunerative. Usually with a big field (it holds the record for races everywhere with 66 runners in 1929) the race is often a chapter of excitement and mishaps with many of the horses failing to negotiate the course. Bookmakers often attempt to attract extra custom by offering permutations on the result of the Grand National, but another way to bet is with the Tote, a government-backed body first instituted by an Act of Parliament in 1928.

The Horserace Totalisator Board (Tote) was established in 1928 as the Racecourse Betting Control Board and the Tote assumed its present name when it was reconstituted in 1961. The Aga Khan wrote a letter to *The Times* in the early 1920's, which sparked off some controversy. He stated his fears for the bloodstock industry because not enough money was being channelled back into racing and horseracing was being run for the benefit of bookmakers. His letter exemplified the feelings of the racing authorities, notably the Jockey Club, and Lord Hamilton of Dalzell, who was one of the prime movers in the campaign to get tote betting legalised.

The Tote first introduced on-course betting facilities as an alternative to bookmakers at Newmarket and Carlisle, in July 1929. Telephone wires which led back to the control room at Newmarket were cut by members of racecourse protection gangs who operated at that time and the marquees which were set up to take bets had to be policed to stop the gangs cutting the guy-ropes. All 70 race courses were covered by 1934.

The Tote method of pooling the total amount staked on a race and then equitably distributing the pool among the winners from a hand operated machine was first used in New Zealand in 1880. But the system was devised earlier by a French chemist named Pierre Oller in the 1860's.

In New Zealand in 1913 an electrical calculator was put into use and in this form the totalisator came to Europe in 1928 when it was tried at France's Longchamp track. The pari-mutuel, as the name indicates (*pari* - wager; *mutuel* - among all) now operates throughout France with Pari-mutuel Urbain (PMU) offices collecting the off-course bets and transmitting them back to the course.

Since this totalisator system depends entirely on the number of bets in the pool, the return dividend can never be exactly gauged until the final bet is made. For the year ending March 1983, 50.2 per cent of Tote returns in Britain were higher than the starting price returned by the bookmakers, and 48.8 per cent were lower.

THE TOTE

The Tote also operate a popular placepot bet at all race meetings and a jackpot, Tote daily double and treble at the major meetings. With their subsidiaries Tote Credit and Tote Bookmakers the Tote's turnover for the year ending March 1983 was just below £110 million.

The placepot consists of naming a horse to finish first, second or third (or fourth in handicaps of 16 or more runners) in each race at one particular meeting. The jackpot which operates at only the major meetings, consists of naming the winner of each race for the first six races. If either are not won they are then carried forward to another meeting and surprise results often lead to lucrative payouts, particularly on the jackpot.

The Tote double is run on the third and fifth races of the day. To win you need to select the winners of both races. The treble is a similar bet but entails picking the successful horse in the second, fourth and sixth races. Permutations of several horses in each race will increase the chance of winning but little profit will be made if short-odds horses win.

BOOKMAKERS AND BETTING SHOPS

Below you will find a comprehensive guide to bets accepted by bookmakers. But before taking advantage of the list it should be stressed that choice of bookmaker is equally important as selections of the day.

Betting shop rules around the country vary enormously and their ceiling for the amount you can win in one day could change your euphoria into total disappointment unless you have first made yourself aware of the bookmaker's rules before placing your bet. For instance, a one-man seaside betting shop makes his money on a seasonal basis with safeguards built into his rules, offsetting any chance of his being made redundant by a holidaymaker he is unlikely to see again. His operation can hardly be compared with that of the major companies who have branches nationwide with rules governing the big cities and less populated areas alike. Even blessed with a dream day it is extremely unlikely that you would exceed their limit.

William Hill, for instance, will pay up to a quarter of a million pounds on the ITV seven (or six) and on their own jackpot bet. But their limit of £100,000 in-a-day far exceeds that of most bookmakers other than Mecca, Coral's, Ladbrokes or other major companies.

Even then the William Hill Organization have an amendment to that rule. Their limit will only be paid out if the horses selected are from meetings covered by Extel (Exchange Telegraph). If not, then £20,000 is the ceiling figure.

Extel provide a 'blower' service to the betting shops and since they usually cover up to five meetings, most days the £100,000 limit applies. But when there are six or more race meetings (particularly on Bank Holidays) failing to find out which meetings are to be covered could prove very costly.

It used to be the case that each sporting newspaper returned their own starting prices and they often differed. But in 1926 they agreed to a uniformed return of starting prices and these are now transmitted back from the racecourse by Extel, who also provide betting shows and commentaries on races.

'First past the post' is another rule that could catch the southerner out when he ventures north. The rule is virtually non-existent in the south, but in some northern betting shops pay-out on first past the post applies regardless of what happens thereafter. Stewards inquiries, objections or failing to weigh in may subsequently change the result, but only the punter who names the horse first past the post will receive his money.

There can also be differences in settling each way doubles, trebles and accumulators. In some betting shops each way bets are settled in such a way that after each selection is calculated, the resulting returns are equally divided between win and place on the next selection. However it is far more common for each way doubles, trebles and accumulators to be settled in separate halves with win money going on to the win selection and place money going on to place selections.

In horse races of five runners or less the place portion of the starting place wager goes on to win as there is no place returned in such races. With six or seven runners, first and second are calculated and with eight runners or more first, second and third are calculated. In handicaps of 16 or more runners first, second, third and fourth are calculated, but this can vary according to the bookmakers' rules.

THE BETS

Every betting shop has its rules. Ask to see them and make sure you are not caught out. No reputable bookmaker will mind your asking, but if he refuses take your business elsewhere. There are thousands to choose from.

A careful study of 'speciality bets' offered by the major companies is also worth careful consideration, with consolation and bonus payments making some look specially attractive. For instance a 'yankee' made up from four selections (which comprises six doubles, four trebles and one fourfold) is probably the country's most popular bet. Add a single bet on each of your four selections and it becomes a 'yap' with just one winner giving you a return on your outlay. But take the 'yap' to a William Hill office and write your selections on their 'Lucky 15' slip and the same bet will double the odds with only one winner and give you a 10 per cent bonus for all four winners.

Most of the leading companies have speciality bets which are usually modifications of bets listed below with extra incentives to attract. Look for value-for-money and take advantage of these offers.

Accumulator

An accumulator is a bet of four or more selections, in which the total returns are invested on to each successive selection. Other common names for accumulators are fourfold (four entries), fivefold (five entries), or roll-up.

Ante-post

Ante-post is a bet normally struck prior to the day of the race on the understanding that if the horse does not run the wager is lost. Exception to the rule is when the selection is balloted out and in such circumstances bets are void and stakes returned.

Banko

Banko is seven bets involving three selections in different events, that is three doubles and one treble plus a roundabout. for example 50p banko A, B and C, total stakes £3.50p.

      3×50p doubles, AB, AC, BC and 50p treble ABC
Plus 50p A any to come £1 double BC
     50p B any to come £1 double AC
     50p C any to come £1 double AB

Canadian (Super Yankee)

Known by either name, this consists of five horses in 26 different combinations of doubles, trebles and accumulators.

CSF See SPSF

Double

A double is a bet involving two selections in which the total return from the first selection is invested onto the second selection.

Double stakes about

A double stakes about consists of two bets involving two selections in different events. For example:
    50p A, 50p B Double stakes about (DSA) total stake £1
    50p A any to come £1 B; 50p B any to come £1 A.

Dundee shuffle

Six bets covering four selections and an any-to-come double on the remaining two.

Fido

The fido consists of 20 bets involving five selections in different events, that is ten doubles and ten trebles.

Flag

A flag is 23 bets involving four selections in different events, that is a Yankee plus the four selections in single stakes about bets.

Goliath

Consists of 247 bets involving eight selections in different events, that is twenty-eight doubles, fifty-six trebles, seventy fourfolds, fifty-six fivefolds, twenty-eight sixfolds, eight sevenfolds and one eightfold.

Heinz

A heinz consists of 57 bets involving six selections in different events, that is 15 doubles, 20 trebles, 15 fourfolds, six fivefolds and one sixfold.

ITV 7 (or 6)

Consists of naming the winner of each of the seven (or six) races televised by ITV. Speciality bets on the ITV Seven are also available from major bookmakers.

Patent

A patent consists of 7 bets involving three selections in different events, that is a single on each selection plus three doubles and a treble.

Reverse Forecast

A simplified method of writing two straight forecasts. That is:
 £1 straight forecast A to beat B plus
 £1 straight forecast B to beat A is equal to
 £1 reversed forecast A and B. Total stake £2.00.

Roundabout

A roundabout consists of three bets involving three selections in different events, that is single any-to-come a double stake double on the remaining two selections, three times.
For example:
 50p roundabout ABC total stake £1.50
 50p A any-to-come £1 double BC
 50p B any-to-come £1 double AC
 50p C any-to-come £1 double AB

Rounder

A rounder consists of three bets involving three selections in different events. That is a single, any-to-come a single stake double on the remaining two selections, three times.
For example:
 50p rounder ABC total stake £1.50
 50p A any-to-come 50p double BC
 50p B any-to-come 50p double AC
 50p C any-to-come 50p double AB

Round Robin

A round robin consists of ten bets involving three selections in different events, that is three pairs of single stakes about bets, (cross bets) plus three doubles and one treble.

Tote returns

To calculate the returns from a tote pool — known as a dividend — the total stake in each pool (less the statutory deduction to cover operational expenses) is divided by the number of winning tickets and a dividend is declared to a fixed stake, for various win, place and forecast pools. Bookmakers wishing to lay bets at tote returns must obtain authorization from the Tote Board, to whom they pay a fee.

Treble

A treble is a bet involving three selections in which the total returns are invested onto each successive selection.

Trixie

A trixie is four bets involving three selections in different events, that is three doubles plus one treble.

With the field

The instruction refers to the fact that the client's selection is coupled with all the entries in the event. For example:
1. A horse with the field in straight forecasts (six runners) - five bets.
2. Daily tote double, three in the first leg with the field in the second leg (eight runners) - 24 bets.

Yankee

A Yankee consists of 11 bets involving four selections in different events, that is six doubles, four trebles and one fourfold.

Yap (yankee patent)

A Yap consists of 15 bets involving four selections in different events, that is a single on each plus a Yankee.

Tricast

Tricast involves naming the 1-2-3 in the correct order in specified handicaps. The starting prices of each horse are then fed into a central computer and the tricast return is formulated.

THE RULES OF RACING

Howard Wright

EARLY HISTORY OF RACING

It is not coincidence that thoroughbred racing in Britain has been dubbed The Sport of Kings. Though there are records of horse racing during the Roman occupation, modern development of an organised sport can be charted through the influence of various monarchs.

In the reign of Henry II (1154-89) there was reference to races at Smoothfield, now known as Smithfield, in London; the sport grew in popularity among the gentry during the time of Richard II (1189-99), and during the reign of Henry VIII (1509-47) the organised establishment of Chester races on the Roodee began the only meeting that is still held at its original location.

James I (1603-25) encouraged the development of racing at Newmarket, an example pursued by his successor, Charles I (1625-49). Following a lull enforced by the arrival of Oliver Cromwell, Charles II (1660-85) restored the fortunes of the sport and his institution of the Town Plate at Newmarket marked the first occasion that rules were written and published for the conduct of a race. The event continues to this day.

William III (1689-1702) founded the Royal Stud at Hampton Court, and Queen Anne (1702-14) was responsible for introducing the Royal Ascot meeting. Thereafter the responsibility for developing racing passed into other hands, though the influence of the monarchy cannot be underestimated.

EMERGENCE OF THE JOCKEY CLUB

The first racing calendar was produced in 1727 by John Cheney of Arundel, who brought out a publication which resembled a form book rather than the present-day Racing Calendar of entries and adjudications. Cheney's work illustrated that, despite its occasional setbacks, racing was being held regularly up and down the country at the time of his death in 1751.

The initial acceptance that a body had assumed some authority for the sport came in 1752, when the name of the Jockey Club first appeared in print, though its precise formation is not known and it had probably been in existence for at least two years.

The fact that the Jockey Club came to govern and reform the Turf was not intended at the time of its formation. It happened largely through the influence of a few individuals, and the fact that the members carried authority by their positions in public life, being in the main either rich or influential, or both.

The first recorded reform by the Jockey Club came in 1756, when it was decided to abolish heats in Jockey Club plates, running one race instead, to create interest. Previously all races were contested in a series of heats and a final, all run on the same day and often over a distance of four miles.

By the time that the first official list of Jockey Club members was published in 1835, the Club's influence had grown. At first its jurisdiction was limited to Newmarket, where its authority was laid down in 1758 with the ruling that every rider taking part there had to weigh in, and anyone 'guilty of contempt of the order of this Club' would not be allowed again to ride at Newmarket.

Gradually it became the practice for disputes at meetings other than Newmarket to be sent to the Jockey Club for a verdict, and in 1816 the Jockey Club recorded its willingness to settle disputes, subject to certain conditions. The most important was that the reference should come through the stewards of the meeting where it arose, thus putting the Jockey Club seal on other fixtures. This was taken an important step further in 1832, when the Jockey Club announced that while its Rules and Orders applied only to Newmarket, other courses were recommended to adopt them and the stewards of the Jockey Club would only consider disputes from courses which had declared in print that their races took place under 'the Rules and Regulations of Newmarket'. Today's organisation of racing in Britain, and its reciprocal arrangements with other nations, dates from that declaration.

RACING CALENDAR

On Cheney's death in 1751 his calendar was succeeded by Heber's Calendar, published by Reginald Heber, and the Sporting Kalendar of Mr Pond. Though Pond had the distinction of publishing the Laws of Racing for the first time in 1751, Heber's publication soon saw off his rival until the author's death in 1769 brought another battle for readership. Walker's volume of that year quickly gave way to the jointly-published Sporting Calendar of William Tuting and Thomas Fawconer, but soon Tuting was persuaded by James Weatherby to break away from his partner. When Tuting died in 1773, James Weatherby produced his first Racing Calendar, and within two years he had beaten off the competition from Fawconer. Since 1778 the Weatherby family have preserved the monopoly of the Racing Calendar, which gradually became the official publication for Jockey Club matters.

James Weatherby's first Racing Calendar contained no

mention of rules for the conduct of racing, but in 1797 they were published for the first time, and appeared with the acknowledgement that they derived from Mr Pond's version as published in his Racing Kalendar for 1751.

In 1828 the Rules and Orders of the Jockey Club were revised and numbered for the first time; and in 1830 Pond's Rules of Horse Racing were also numbered. Pond's influence lasted until April 19, 1858, when a new set of rules covering 66 sections was introduced following the report of a Jockey Club committee.

Another Jockey Club committee met in 1870 to consider the rules and a number of alterations were made, but the next major overhaul came at the beginning of 1877, after a further committee had redrawn the rule book and all previous legislation was repealed. These lasted until the start of 1890, when the forerunner of the modern rule book was introduced, with better lay-out and index and more comprehensive coverage in its 186 sections. This stayed in operation, with various amendments, until 1969.

THREE INFLUENTIAL FIGURES

Sir Charles Bunbury (1740-1821) MP for Suffolk for 43 years and a steward of the Jockey Club at the age of 28, he was a prominent owner who won the first running of the Derby with Diomed (1780). Two-year-old racing and the five Classics (1,000 Guineas, 2,000 Guineas, Derby, Oaks and St Leger) were established during his time, and he was particularly active in encouraging the racing of younger horses over shorter distances.

Lord George Bentinck (1802-48) A prolific owner and a heavy gambler, he did not always foil the bookmakers as he did when transporting Elis in a specially-constructed horse-box for the 1836 St Leger, at a time when most horses were walked to race meetings. His chief success as a Turf reformer came in making racing better organised for the public and tackling the spread of villainy. He introduced the numbering of horses, better starting and the parading of horses; he also developed the racecourse at Goodwood. He exposed the fraud of Running Rein, first past the post in the 1844 Derby but subsequently revealed to be a four-year-old called Maccabaeus.

Admiral Henry John Rous (1791-1877) First elected a steward of the Jockey Club in 1838, he became the most noted of all Turf administrators. Having begun the reorganisation of the Jockey Club's financial position, he became a brilliant handicapper and drew up the weight-for-age scale, detailing how much weight young horses should receive from older opponents over different distances, that was used until 1973.

THE NATIONAL HUNT COMMITTEE

Development of steeplechasing in the first half of the 19th Century, bringing the first Steeplechasing Calendar of Henry Wright in 1845, led to a movement to establish a code of conduct distinct from the rules and regulations of the Jockey Club. Mr BJ Angell, a prominent owner, and Mr W G Craven, a member of the Jockey Club, made the first tentative moves to set up a proper organisation and with the help of Lord Grey de Wilton they formed a National Hunt Committee which had its first recorded meeting in 1866.

New rules of the National Hunt Committee were introduced in 1877, and lasted until 1894, when re-drafting brought in a comprehensive set more in line with the Jockey Club version. These largely remained in use until 1954.

Within two years of its centenary, the National Hunt Committee had disappeared. The call for streamlining of racing's administration led to amalgamation of the Jockey Club and National Hunt Committee in 1968, and the new ruling body was to be known as the Jockey Club.

To accompany amalgamation, one set of rules was drawn up to cover both Flat and National Hunt racing, and this enabled a complete overhaul of the rules to take place.

1969 REORGANISATION OF THE RULES

Differences in the order and make-up of the rules between Flat racing and National Hunt were ironed out at the beginning of 1969, and the rule book was brought into the second half of the 20th Century. The idea was to divide the rules into broad outlines to bring in a definite and recognisable order.

THE RULES (in essence)

STEWARDS

The stewards of the Jockey Club grant licences to racecourses, officials, jockeys, trainers and valets. They fix the dates on which race meetings are held, and they impose penalties on those found guilty of breaking the rules. They do not enter into disputes or claims relating to bets, but they are allowed 'to exercise any other powers conferred on them by these rules and to take any such action as they consider necessary for the purposes of carrying out or putting into effect these rules'. Their word is the law in racing.

Stewards of race meetings are appointed by each racecourse and have to be approved by the Jockey Club stewards. There must be at least four at each meeting — five if there are nine races or more — and they make whatever arrangements are thought necessary for the conduct of the meeting. They alone have the power to abandon racing. Their disciplinary powers are limited. Cases in which they regard the breach of the rules to be beyond their scope, are referred to the Jockey Club stewards.

OFFICIALS

Clerk of the Course: is appointed by each racecourse to be responsible for the conduct of the meetings with special regard for the condition of the course. He will also be closely concerned with the framing of the race conditions.

Clerk of the Scales: weighs the riders before each race, weighs the riders of the first four horses placed by the judge after the race, and notifies the stewards of any discrepancies. He is also responsible for the official notification of accidents during a race, all fines inflicted by the stewards and details of horses sold or claimed.

Handicappers: allot weights to be carried in a handicap race so that each horse in theory has an equal chance. Weights are published in the Racing Calendar and only by permission of the Jockey Club stewards can they be changed. They are required to attend race meetings under instructions from the Jockey Club stewards.

Inspector of courses: inspects every licensed racecourse periodically to review safety standards and the provisions of the Jockey Club's Racecourse Guidelines (Fixed Equipment).

Judge: places the first six horses in order of passing the winning-post. His decision is final, though he may correct a mistake, but it is subject to the powers of the Jockey Club stewards.

Stakeholder: collects all entrance fees for runners and other sums due under the condition of the races, and 15 days after a meeting makes the payments relating to the prize money for each race.

Starter: controls the horses and riders at the start, from where he dispatches the field for each race, ensuring a fair start. He may withdraw a horse at the start, and can declare a false start if there is any faulty action of the starting stalls or starting gate. A race started in front of the starting post, or on a wrong course, or before the appointed time is void.

Stewards' secretary: assists the stewards with advice relating to the conduct of the meeting and the rules of racing.

HORSES

Horses take their age from January 1 in the year they are born, and have done so since 1834, when the May 1 rule was altered. Names must be registered with the Racing Calendar Office, and after a certificate of age and marking has been approved, each horse is issued with a passport to verify identification and vaccination.

OWNERS

All owners must be registered by the Jockey Club stewards. It is possible for horses to be owned by recognised clubs and companies, syndicates (of not more than 12 persons) and partnerships.

TRAINERS

Every trainer must obtain from the Jockey Club stewards a licence, or a permit in the case of one training a National Hunt horse for himself and certain specified relatives.

RIDERS

No-one under the age of 16 can ride under Jockey Club rules, and each rider must obtain from the Jockey Club stewards a licence as a flat-race jockey or apprentice jockey, or a steeplechase and hurdle race jockey or conditional jockey, or a permit to ride as an amateur jockey. Apprenticeship ends on attaining the age of 24.

RACECOURSES

Every racecourse must be licensed annually by the Jockey Club stewards, and it is their duty to comply with Jockey Club guidelines and publish a daily official card of the races and their conditions and runners. All meetings must be authorised by the Jockey Club stewards.

PROGRAMMES OF RACES

The conditions of every race before entries close and the full programme of every meeting before it takes place must be published in the Racing Calendar, showing dates for closing, declaration of forfeit, publication of the weights for handicaps and timing of penalties after closing. No horse under the age of two is allowed to run, and no race can be less than five furlongs. There are further restrictions on the type of races permitted on any one day, and there are special conditions for weights in handicaps so that top weight in Flat races is either 10 stone or 9 st 7 lb and bottom weight 7 st 7 lb.

In selling races the winner is offered for auction at a stipulated minimum price, over which any surplus is divided between the owner of the winner and the racecourse executive according to a stated scale of percentages. All other horses in a selling race, or all those in a claiming race, may be claimed for a stipulated minimum price.

PENALTIES AND ALLOWANCES

Race conditions may allow for penalties or allowances according to prize money won in previous races, but the winner of a race confined to apprentice jockeys on the Flat does not acquire a penalty in future races, unless specifically stated in the race conditions.

The holder of an apprentice jockey's licence may claim the following weight allowances in all handicaps and selling races and all other races with guaranteed prize money of not more than £3,500: 7 lb until they have won 10 Flat races, thereafter 5 lb until they have won 50 Flat races, and thereafter 3 lb until they have won 75 Flat races, and in all cases apprentice races are not included in the totals.

ENTRIES

All entries must be made in writing by the owner of the horse or his authorised agent, and in most races the closing of entries takes place no more than 23 days before the start of the meeting for which the races are advertised. Entries for races with guaranteed prize money of more than £8,000 may close before this period.

DECLARATIONS AND SCRATCHINGS

In every race there is a declaration of runners either four or three days before the race. In those races which close more than 23 days before the race there is provision for one or two stages at which forfeit may be declared, and only in these can scratchings be made by the owner or his authorised agent. Declaration of a runner is made before a stipulated time on the day preceding the race.

If at the time fixed for cancellations the number of horses remaining engaged is greater than the recommended safety factor, the number is reduced by dividing the race into more than one part, or in the case of a handicap by eliminating horses from the bottom of the handicap upwards, or in certain major races by eliminating those horses which the Jockey Club handicapper regards as having the lowest ratings, until the safety requirement is met.

LIABILITY FOR ENTRANCE MONEY

The nominator and every owner of the horse at the time of nomination are liable for paying the initial entrance fee and any other sums due under the conditions of a race. An 'Unpaid Forfeit' List is maintained and published in the Racing Calendar six times a year, showing arrears notified by the stakeholder of any meeting, and until these arrears are paid, a horse cannot be entered or started for a race.

WEIGHING OUT

The name of the race, horse and rider must be given in writing to the clerk of the course not less than 45 minutes before the time fixed for the race, after which the rider may be weighed out by the clerk of the scales. It is the trainer's responsibility to see that the rider carries the correct weight, and no rider may be weighed out less than 15 minutes before the time of the race. The rider weighs out with everything the horse will carry except skull cap, whip, bridle, rings, plates and anything worn on the horse's legs.

The rider is responsible for the fit condition of his saddle, except in the case of an apprentice or where a stable employee rides for the trainer who employs him, when the trainer is responsible.

A rider must weigh out with any hood, blinkers or eyeshield the horse will wear and which have to be declared at the overnight stage of the race.

RUNNING OF RACES

Every horse which runs in a race shall run on its merits, and every rider must obtain the best possible placing. Trainers have a duty to give the proper instructions to their jockeys. Jockeys found guilty of careless, improper or reckless riding which causes interference to another runner are liable to suspension.

If only one horse is declared to run, it need not 'walk over' the entire course, but must be ridden past the judge's box as if crossing the winning line. When horses run a dead heat, the owners divide the prize money for the placings, but each horse which dead heats for first place shall be regarded as having won outright for the purposes of determining penalties.

WEIGHING-IN

The riders of the horses placed first, second and third must unsaddle at a place appointed by the course, but all jockeys must present themselves to be weighed in after the race. Normally the clerk of the scales will require only the first four jockeys to be weighed in. If a rider weighs in at more than 2 lb over the weight at which he weighed out, he is reported to the stewards; if he cannot draw the weight at which he weighed out, and is more than 1 lb out, his horse is disqualified.

DISPUTES

The time limits for disputes and objections vary from a period up to 10.30am on the day of the race for an objection to a horse engaged in a race that day, to within five minutes of the winner being weighed in or the judge having announced the placings, whichever is the later, for an objection arising from the running of the race itself. Objections on other grounds may be made within 14 days of the meeting's close. In cases of fraud or wilful mis-statement, there is no time limit.

Objections have to be made in writing, accompanied by a deposit which is forfeited if the case goes against the claimant, unless the stewards feel there was good cause for the objection. Every objection is decided by three stewards. Appeals may be made against penalties imposed by stewards of local meetings on application to the Jockey Club stewards.

DISQUALIFICATION OF HORSES

Horses are not qualified to be entered or started if they have run at a meeting not recognised by the Jockey Club, or are in the ownership of a disqualified person, or are the product of artificial insemination. They are not qualified to start for a race if they have not been entered or declared properly, or have been tubed on the day of the race, or the vaccination details on their passports do not match the Jockey Club requirements, or if for the 14 days prior to the race they have not been in the care of or trained by a licensed trainer.

DISTRIBUTION OF PRIZES

Prize money is distributed according to a complicated formula of percentages that allows for sums to be paid direct to various sources through the Jockey Club agents, Weatherbys, rather than be left to the discretion of the winning owner. Varying percentages go to the owner, trainer, jockey and stable associated with at least the first three placed horses, and in certain races also to the fourth. In all races 0.20 per cent is allotted each to the apprentice training scheme and the Jockeys' Valets' attendance fund.

In the majority of Flat races, with three prizes, the distribution is: 54 per cent to the owner of the winner; 17 per cent to the owner of second; 8.5 per cent to the owner of third; 7 per cent to the trainer of winner; 1 per cent to the trainer of second; 0.5 per cent to the trainer of third; 5.23 per cent to the jockey who rode winner; 0.93 per cent to the jockey who rode second; 0.44 per cent to the jockey who rode third; 3.5 per cent to the stable from which winner trained; 1 per cent to the stable from which second trained; 0.5 per cent to the stable from which third trained; 0.2 per cent to apprentice training; 0.2 per cent to Jockeys' Valets' attendance fund.

DISQUALIFICATION OF PERSONS

The Jockey Club stewards will declare anyone a disqualified
person if he tries to or succeeds in administering a prohibited
substance to a horse; or tries to or succeeds in bribing anyone
having anything to do with the official side of racing.
Conversely, anyone on the official side who succumbs to
either temptation is liable to be declared a disqualified
person.

A disqualified person cannot act as a steward or authorised
agent; he cannot enter, run, train or ride a horse at an
authorised meeting; normally he cannot work in a racing
stable, and under no circumstances can he act as a dealer in a
horse intended for racing, or go on any racecourse operating
under Jockey Club rules.

JOCKEY CLUB INSTRUCTIONS

Stewards of the Jockey Club publish various instructions in the
Racing Calendar from time to time, and while not
incorporated into the rules, they have the same weight. These
instructions are more advisory in nature, but in time they may
be framed into rules.

CHANGES TO RULES AND INSTRUCTIONS

Before 1969, intended rule changes had to go to the Jockey
Club as a recommendation from the stewards; they went on to
rules committee for debate and back to the Jockey Club for
approval; and they were finally confirmed at a further Jockey
Club meeting. It took about three months to get a rule
changed. Since 1969 rule changes have been brought into
effect immediately after modification and publication in the
Racing Calendar. In March each year all changes made during
a year are published in one paper, and approved by a Jockey
Club meeting in time for the Flat season.

Rule changes may be suggested from many sources —
disciplinary hearings, licence applications, policy
amendments, court cases, race-planning meetings,
racecourse officials, government decisions. But whatever the
source, the rules of racing are never static.

WEIGHT-FOR-AGE

Racehorses begin racing in most cases as two-year-olds. Horses achieve the status of two-year-olds on January 1 in the second year after their birth. With the foaling season extending from January to June or even July, it is clear that when the Flat-race season begins in late March, two-year-olds are still immature animals.

In the middle of the last century, Admiral Rous, one of the most influential figures in the Jockey Club, formulated a scale of weight-for-age which reflected the relationship between the relative maturity of horses of various ages with respect to distance.

The scale, revised by Admiral Rous in 1873, expressed the weights to be carried by horses of differing ages at the various distances over which they might meet at progressive stages of the season (March to November).

Few races in the first half of the season allow for competition between two-year-olds and their seniors, but the scale of weight-for-age, which was again modified in 1976, is most useful for the laying down of relative weights to be carried by three-year-olds against their seniors.

The longer the distance, the greater is the weight advantage.

Distance	Age	MARCH APRIL		MAY		JUNE	
		Mar & Apr 1-15	16-30	1-15	16-31	1-15	16-30
5 Furlongs	2	32	31	29	27	26	25
	3	13	12	11	10	9	8
6 Furlongs	2	—	—	30	29	29	28
	3	15	14	13	12	11	10
7 Furlongs	2	—	—	—	—	—	—
	3	16	15	14	13	12	11
1 Mile	2	—	—	—	—	—	—
	3	18	17	16	15	14	13
9 Furlongs	3	18	17	16	15	14	13
1¼ Miles	3	19	18	17	16	15	14
11 Furlongs	3	20	19	18	17	16	15
1½ Miles	3	20	19	18	17	16	15
13 Furlongs	3	21	20	19	18	17	16
1¾ Miles	3	21	20	19	18	17	16
15 Furlongs	3	22	21	20	19	18	17
2 Miles	3	22	21	20	19	18	17
2¼ Miles	3	23	22	21	20	19	18
2½ Miles	3	25	24	23	22	21	20

The later in the year, the narrower becomes the
gap. The scale of weight-for-age is published with the full
authority of the Jockey Club to help clerks of the course in the
framing of the conditions of races.

Because it is considered that two-year-olds are immature,
no two-year-old may race over further than five furlongs until
mid-May. Late June is the earliest date for seven-furlong
races, and two-year-olds cannot tackle a mile before August.
The few mile and a quarter races for juveniles are staged at
the end of the season.

SCALE OF WEIGHT-FOR-AGE

*The scale of weight-for-age is published by authority of the
Stewards of the Jockey Club as a guide to Clerks of Courses in
the framing of races. It is founded on the scale published by
Admiral Rous and revised by him in 1873. It has been modified
in accordance with suggestions from the principal trainers and
practical authorities; it has been further revised since and
republished in 1976 in its present form.*

**Allowance, assessed in lbs, which 3 years old will receive from 4 years
old, and 2 years old will receive from 3 years old**

JULY		AUG		SEPT		OCT		NOV
1-15	16-31	1-15	16-31	1-15	16-30	1-15	16-31	
25	23	21	20	19	18	17	16	15
7	6	5	4	3	2	1	—	—
27	26	26	24	22	21	21	20	18
9	8	7	6	5	4	3	2	1
—	—	—	—	24	23	23	22	21
10	9	8	7	6	5	4	3	2
—	—	—	—	27	27	26	25	24
12	11	10	9	8	7	6	5	4
12	11	10	9	8	7	6	5	4
13	12	11	10	9	8	7	6	5
14	13	12	11	10	9	8	7	6
14	13	12	11	10	9	8	7	6
15	14	13	12	11	10	9	8	7
15	14	13	12	11	10	9	8	7
16	15	14	13	12	11	10	9	8
16	15	14	13	12	11	10	9	8
17	16	15	14	13	12	11	10	9
19	18	17	16	15	14	13	12	11

GLOSSARY OF TERMS

Adrian Hunt

Added money Money added to the overall prize money for a race by the racecourse executive or any other source.
All-out When a horse is doing its maximum at the end of a race.
Also-ran Any horse which does not reach the first four places in a race.
Amateur rider Unpaid rider who holds a permit from the Jockey Club to compete in races as such.
Apprentice Learner-jockey; a rider who is younger than 24 years old. Apprentices get a weight allowance of 7 lb, 5 lb, or 3 lb depending on the number of winners they have ridden.
Auction race Event restricted to horses which have been sold at public auction, the cheaper ones usually getting a weight concession from the more expensive buys.
Autumn double The Cambridgeshire Handicap and the Cesarewitch Handicap, both run at Newmarket.

Balloted out Horses at the bottom of the handicap which have been eliminated from a race because the field exceeds the safety limit.
Bandage Protective binding around the lower part of a horse's leg.
Birthday-January 1 All horses, regardless of the month in which they were born, become officially one year older every January 1st.
Blaze Large white marking on horse's face.
Blinkers Eye-coverings designed so that the horse can see only what is directly in front.
Bloodstock Horses which are bred for racing.
Blower Telephone link between bookmakers on and off the course operated by the Exchange Telegraph Company.
Break down Go lame.
Breeder The person who owned the dam at the time its son or daughter was born.
Bloodmare A mare kept for breeding purposes.
Brothers and sisters Horses which have the same sire and dam.
Bumpers' race Events confined to amateur riders.

Camera patrol Film of a race, operated by Racecourse Technical Services, to assist the stewards in any inquiry.
Canter Half-speed gallop.
Cast A horse in such a position that it cannot stand up in its box.
Claim Weight allowance received by an apprentice or amateur rider when competing against professional jockeys.
Claiming race Race in which any of the runners may be claimed (bought) for a set amount of money.
Classics The 1,000 Guineas, 2,000 Guineas, Derby, Oaks and St Leger.
Clerk of the Course Licensed official responsible for the general running of a race meeting.
Clerk of the Scales Licensed official responsible for ensuring that each runner carries the correct weight.
Colours (of horses) There are seven main colourings for horses;

B=bay, Br=brown, Bl=black, Gr=grey, Ro=roan,
Ch=chestnut, Wh=white.
Colt A male entire horse under the age of five.
Conditions races Non-handicaps.
Crib biting When a horse seizes any object in the stable, arches
its neck and swallows repeatedly.
Cup races Conditions races for stayers, for example Ascot Gold,
Doncaster, Goodwood, Jockey Club and Yorkshire Cups.

Dam A horse's mother
Dead weight Amount of lead added to weight cloth to make up
difference between weight of jockey and weight the horse
must carry in a race.
Declared overnight Horse confirmed as a definite starter by its
owner or trainer the day before a race.
Distance 1 Margin announced by the Judge, which exceeds
30 lengths.   2 The "distance" marker at a racecourse is a
point 240 yards before the winning post.
Divided race Non-handicap, usually of low value, which is split
into two or more parts to comply with the safety limit.
Dope test Samples of saliva, urine or blood taken from a horse
for examination.
Draw The stall number, declared overnight, from which a horse
must start.
Dropped his hands When a jockey eases his mount down; either
when it is winning easily or being well beaten.

Entire A male horse who has not been gelded.
Entries All horses originally entered for a given race, some of
which drop out at various acceptance and declaration stages.

Favourite Horse which starts at shortest price in a race.
Field All the runners in a race.
Filly Female horse under the age of five.
Firing When hot irons or acid are applied to a horse's legs to
strengthen tendons after injury.
Foal Any horse which has not reached its first birthday.
Forfeit list A list, published in the Racing Calendar, of persons
who have defaulted in their financial racing obligations.
Form Previous performances of a horse.
Free handicap One in which no liability for stakes or forfeit is
incurred until acceptance.

Gelding Male horse which has been castrated.
General Stud Book A volume first published in 1793 and updated
every four years. Published by Weatherbys, it contains the
pedigrees of all thoroughbred horses.
Girth The band placed around the centre of a horse's body to
keep the saddle in place.
Going State of the ground. Terms used are hard, firm, good to
firm, good, good to soft (or yielding), soft, heavy.
Got a leg When a horse has a swollen leg or is lame.

Got at Outside interference to a horse before a race to ruin its chance of winning, usually by administration of drugs (dope).
Grand £1,000.
Green Inexperienced — mainly applied to a horse's running.
Group race See **pattern race.**

Half-brothers or sisters Horses which have the same dam, but a different sire.
Hand Distance, taken from the highest point of the withers to the ground, by which the height of horses is measured; one hand is equivalent to four inches.
Handicap Race in which the weights carried are framed to give each horse an equal chance of winning.
Hanging When a horse does not race in a straight line.
Hobday Operation, named after its inventor, to improve a horse's breathing.
Hood Full covering of a horse's head. See **blinkers.**
Horse A male entire horse aged five years or more.

International classification Theoretical handicap of the leading horses from England, Ireland and France.
In the frame Any horse which finishes in the first four in a race.
Irons Stirrups in which jockey places his feet while riding.

Jockey Professional rider older than 24.
Jockey Club Ruling body of racing in Great Britain.
Judge Official responsible for establishing the correct order of the first six to finish in each race.

Lad Employee of either sex helping the trainer at his stables.
Laying off Practice among bookmakers who wish to minimise their liabilities on certain horses by backing them with other bookmakers.
Length Distance used by the Judge when placing horses. It is a distance of about eight feet, the approximate length of a horse.
Levy Board Government appointed body which collects money from bookmakers to be used for the benefit of racing.
Listed race Important races which do not have Group or Pattern status and include handicaps.
Long handicap The weights in handicaps normally range from 10 stone to 7 st 7 lb, but some horses are rated below 7 st 7 lb and any mark below that is known as their long handicap weight.

Made all Led throughout a race.
Maiden A horse which has yet to win a race.
Mare Female horse aged five years or older.
Members' Enclosure Racecourse enclosure for people who pay an annual membership fee to a certain course; day badges can be purchased.
Middle-distance Races between 1 mile 1 furlong and 1 mile 5 furlongs.
Monkey £500.

Neck Distance used by the Judge when placing horses—roughly one quarter of a length.
Nobbled See **got at.**
Noseband Sheepskin covering placed round horse's nose so that it keeps its head down while racing.
Number Board Information board showing the runners and riders for a race and, later, the result.
Number cloth Cloth below saddle which displays a horse's racecard number.
Nursery Handicap for two-year-olds.

Objection Protest lodged by a rider who considers that another horse in the race has been involved in an infringement of the Rules of Racing.
Odds-on When the bettor or punter stands to win a smaller amount than his stake.
Off the bit When a horse is not going well and has to be hard ridden by the jockey.
On the bit A horse travelling well and freely with no undue exertion by the jockey.
Outsider Horse which is a big price in the betting.
Owner(s) Persons or companies in whose name a horse is registered.

Pace Speed at which a race is run.
Pacemaker Horse which runs from the front, sometimes to ensure that the race is run to suit his better-fancied stable-companion.
Paddock or Parade Ring Area in which the horses are walked around in public before a race.
Passport A horse's identity book, containing details of its markings and vaccination dates.
Pattern Races Major non-handicap races of Britain, Ireland, France, West Germany and Italy. They are divided into Groups ranging from Group 1 (the best races) to Group 3.
Pedigree A horse's family tree.
Penalty Fixed amount of extra weight which a horse must carry for a recent win if the handicappers have not had time to reassess its chances. Penalties vary depending on the value of the race the horse won.
Penalty value Total prize money earned by a winning horse, the big percentage of which goes to the owner.
Photo-finish A camera fixed on the winning line to assist the Judge in deciding the order of finish. A photo for win or place is called for when the margin is thought to be a neck or less.
Placed A horse which finishes in the first four.
Plate 1 A horse's shoe.
     2 Saddle.
Plater A horse which runs in selling races.
Pony £25.
Post (At the) The starting point of a race.
Post (Winning) The finish of a race.

Puller A horse which is headstrong.
Punter Bettor on races.

Racegoers Club Formed in 1968 by the Racecourse Association, it is a club whose members enjoy financial discounts at certain racemeetings and have the benefit of attending film shows, lectures and organised trips to overseas meetings.
Racing Calendar Official publication of the Jockey Club, listing entries and weights for future races and results of Stewards inquiries.
Rails 1 The running rails which mark the shape of the running course.
2 The barrier between the Members' and Tattersalls enclosures.
Retainer A set fee paid for a particular jockey's services by either a trainer or an owner.
Riding work Partnering a horse in an exercise gallop at his home stables.
Rig A male horse with only one testicle.
Ringer A horse which is substituted for another—sometimes by mistake, sometimes through dishonesty.
Rules of Racing (The) The 'Law' which was laid down by the Jockey Club in 1890 and is constantly revised.

Safety limit The maximum number of runners allowed for one race at a certain course.
Scales Machinery on which the jockeys and their equipment are weighed before and after a race.
Scratched Withdrawn.
Selling race A race in which the winner is put up for public auction immediately afterwards.
Sex allowance Female horses are normally given a weight advantage when competing against males. The usual difference is 3lb but this can vary.
Shoes See **plate.**
Silks Tunic and cap worn by the jockey and displaying the colours of the horse's owner(s).
Silver Ring Cheapest public enclosure at a racecourse.
Sire A horse's father.
Skull cap Protective headgear worn by a jockey under his cap.
Socks Large white-coloured areas just above a horse's feet.
Spring Double The Lincoln Handicap and the Grand National.
Sprints Races over five and six furlongs.
Starter Licensed official responsible for ensuring that all the runners in a race get away to an equal start.
Starting price The price of a horse in the betting when the race starts.
Starting stalls Enclosures, or traps, from which horses are despatched at the start of a race.
Stayer A horse which normally runs in races over 1 mile 6 furlongs or beyond.

"They're off"

Stewards Unpaid officials appointed by the Jockey Club who enforce the Rules of Racing both on the course and off.
Stewards inquiry Investigation by the Stewards.
Stipendiary Steward A steward's secretary who is licensed by the Jockey Club and paid a fee to assist the stewards.
Straight in front A conformation fault between a horse's fetlock and hoof which can lead to lameness.
String The horses in a trainer's stables.
Sweepstake Any race in which the prize money is distributed among the winner and placed horses.

Tattersalls A private sales company based at Newmarket.
Tattersalls Committee The body responsible for dealing with all matters connected with betting.
Tattersalls Ring Main public enclosure at a racecourse.
Thoroughbred Horse whose pedigree is recorded in the General Stud Book.
Tic-Tac Sign language by which bookmakers communicate on a racecourse.
Tote (The) Betting system in which the dividends are controlled by the volume of money wagered.
Tout Old expression and name given to person who watches horses working at home and passes on reports about them (either good or bad) to the press or bookmaker.
Trainer Male or female person holding a licence from the Jockey Club to train racehorses.
Triple Crown Classic treble of the 2,000 Guineas, Derby and St. Leger.
Tubed Operation on horse's throat to improve its breathing—a metal tube is inserted into the neck.
Two-Year-Old A colt, filly or gelding aged two.

Under orders Horses are under (starters) orders when the starter orders a white flag to be raised just before despatching the runners.

Under pressure When a horse is being asked to produce its maximum near the finish. See **all-out.**

Unplaced See **also-ran.**

Unsaddling enclosure Placed horses in a race must be ridden into the unsaddling enclosure which is situated near the weighing room. The horses are unsaddled and their jockeys must immediately "weigh in".

Unsound Horse which is prone to lameness.

Upsides A horse racing alongside another.

Valet Person responsible for looking after and laying out a jockey's equipment at a racemeeting.

Virus Contagious ailment which can affect every horse in a trainer's stable.

Walk-over If only one horse arrives at the racecourse to run in a certain race, it is allowed to "walk-over"—canter past the stands in order to collect the prize money.

Warned off Sentence (of varying degrees) passed by the Stewards of the Jockey Club to punish an offender by barring him from racecourses or withdrawing any licence he may hold.

Weatherbys Messrs Weatherby and Sons are a private family firm who act as agents for the Jockey Club. They deal with much of the administration work connected with racing and are responsible among other things for the publication of the Racing Calendar, the acceptance of entries for declarations for all races, and the registration of owners and their colours.

Weaver Weaving is a nervous habit to which some horses are prone. Weavers are inclined to pace up and down their boxes and/or move their forelegs and heads from side to side for lengthy periods.

Weighed in The jockey and his saddle are weighed directly after a race to ensure the correct weight has been carried.

Weighed out The jockey and his saddle are weighed before a race to ensure that the correct weight is about to be carried.

Weighing Room Room near the unsaddling enclosure in which the scales are situated.

Weight The set amount carried by each horse in a race.

Weight-cloth If the jockey is too light to make the weight the horse must carry, a weight cloth containing lead weights is placed under the horses's saddle.

Weight-for-age A range of weights designed to offset the advantage older horses have over two and three-year-olds when meeting them in condition races. The weight concession decreases as the season progresses and the younger horses become more mature physically.

Whip Part of a jockey's equipment used for urging a horse on or preventing it from hanging in a certain direction.

Winner's enclosure See **unsaddling enclosure.**

Yearling Thoroughbred aged between one year and two.